# INTERGENERATIONAL TRAUMA WORKBOOK

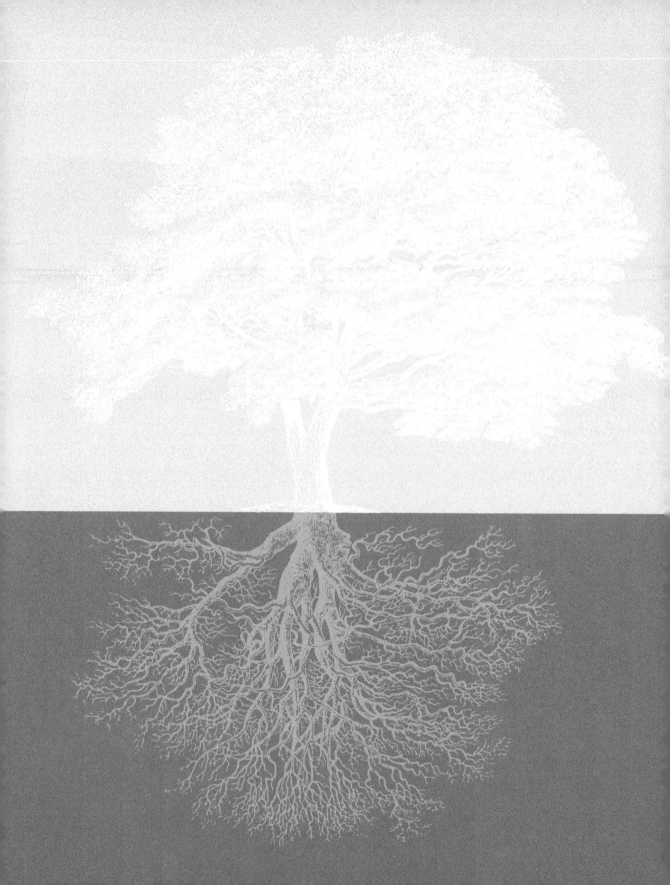

# INTERGENERATIONAL
# TRAUMA
# WORKBOOK

### Strategies to Support Your Journey of Discovery, Growth, and Healing

LYNNE FRIEDMAN-GELL, PHD,
and JOANNE BARRON, PSYD

ROCKRIDGE
PRESS

For general information on our other products and services or to obtain technical support, please contact our Customer Care Department within the United States at (866) 744-2665, or outside the United States at (510) 253-0500.

Rockridge Press publishes its books in a variety of electronic and print formats. Some content that appears in print may not be available in electronic books, and vice versa.

TRADEMARKS: Rockridge Press and the Rockridge Press logo are trademarks or registered trademarks of Callisto Media Inc. and/or its affiliates, in the United States and other countries, and may not be used without written permission. All other trademarks are the property of their respective owners. Rockridge Press is not associated with any product or vendor mentioned in this book.

Interior and Cover Designer: Jennifer Hsu
Art Producer: Samantha Ulban
Editor: Seth Schwartz
Production Editor: Sigi Nacson
Production Manager: Martin Worthington

Illustration © Graphic Goods/Creative Market. All Photography used under license Shutterstock.
Author photos courtesy Cathryn Farnsworth Photography

ISBN: Print 978-1-64739-954-2
eBook 978-1-64739-564-3
R0

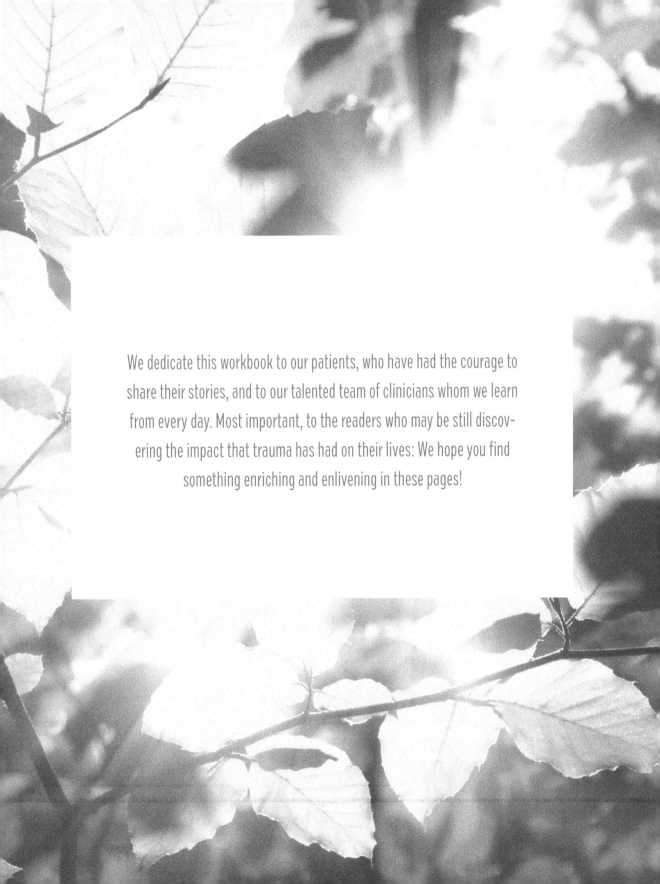

We dedicate this workbook to our patients, who have had the courage to share their stories, and to our talented team of clinicians whom we learn from every day. Most important, to the readers who may be still discovering the impact that trauma has had on their lives: We hope you find something enriching and enlivening in these pages!

# CONTENTS

# INTRODUCTION

Welcome. If you're reading this book, you most likely have experienced trauma, or perhaps recognized it in someone you love. Trauma and its impact on our mental, emotional, and physical well-being has become more and more recognized in the field of psychology in recent years. We believe that understanding intergenerational trauma in particular is key for healing many whose symptoms may have previously been misdiagnosed or misunderstood. We hope you will find the information in this workbook a helpful start to your healing experience.

As clinical psychologists specializing in the treatment of trauma, our understanding of intergenerational trauma has been influenced by over 20 years of trauma studies, as well as our own personal journeys studying with some eminent scholars and teachers in the trauma field.

We have been especially influenced by psychologist Allan Schore, PhD, and our continued studies with him. As informed by Dr. Schore, we believe that technique is not as important as the implicit right-brain to right-brain connection between patient and therapist in promoting growth and healing.

Our own personal histories of intergenerational trauma have also informed our work. Our lived experiences of healing from trauma and finding an increased capacity to live more authentically and joyously lie at the heart of our desire to bring this possibility to others. We opened our treatment program, Trauma and Beyond Psychological Center®, because we wanted to share both our understanding of trauma treatment and the gifts of life *beyond* trauma with those who come to us for help. This workbook is our next step in sharing the opportunities to heal and grow.

Each chapter in this workbook explains an aspect of intergenerational trauma and offers related tools and techniques to empower you to repair, recover, and grow. We'll start with the basics, defining intergenerational and other types of trauma; we'll explore ways to recognize trauma symptoms and understand their connection to your thoughts, beliefs, emotions, and sensations. You'll learn methods for regulating your mood, healing relationships with yourself and others, and finding support as you keep moving forward toward a life of self-growth and more aliveness.

We've designed this book to be a workbook in the truest sense; it's your work that will complete this book. You'll find practical exercises, assessments, reflections, and affirmations with space provided so you can write directly in these pages, creating a record of your progress that you can use as a reference whenever you need it. You'll also find vignettes and real-world examples of the various ways that intergenerational trauma can be experienced in real life. These stories are composites based on clients we've known over the years, with personal details changed. Everyone's story is unique, but we hope some of them will resonate for you.

It's important to note that this workbook can't replace therapy. We encourage anyone who's experiencing symptoms of unresolved trauma to seek help from a therapist. Reading about intergenerational trauma or practicing the exercises and assignments in this workbook may bring up unfamiliar or uncomfortable feelings and emotions, but you don't have to do this alone. If you're not currently receiving therapeutic support, this book's final chapter and resource list provide some guidance in finding therapy and other help.

The journey of healing can be both difficult and amazing. Healing is not linear, and it takes time. Healing is a marathon, not a sprint. But it's a journey well worth taking. The discoveries you're about to make, and the knowledge you will gain, can bring you relief from your trauma symptoms. But we encourage you to go further, to go *beyond* what you have previously thought possible. We're all born with an innate capacity for love, connection, and aliveness. As you heal from intergenerational trauma, this capacity can be awakened and strengthened. Not only can you feel better, but you can also find self-love and love for others and the world. As you move *beyond* your trauma, our hope is that you will be able to feel expansion, aliveness, and more joy in your life.

Now let's begin!

# CHAPTER 1

# UNDERSTANDING INTERGENERATIONAL TRAUMA

If the term *intergenerational trauma* is new to you—even if you've been dealing with your own trauma for a long time—that's not surprising. Though first written about in the mid-1960s, it's only in recent years that intergenerational trauma has become recognized by the mental health community as having deep connections to many emotional and physical issues.

Knowledge is empowering, so this workbook will clarify the concept of intergenerational trauma and its impact on your sense of self, your relationships with others, and the way you experience the world. But more important, in these pages you'll find exercises and tools to support you in your personal journey of discovery and healing. You'll read vignettes and real-life examples of how intergenerational trauma operates in people's lives, and how it can be overcome. This book isn't meant to take the place of therapy, but we think you'll find the contents to be important and helpful for your journey toward healing.

Our starting point is to deepen your understanding. We'll begin with an explanation of intergenerational trauma itself, including how it's transmitted from one generation to the next, and how it might manifest itself in your life. And once you're grounded with that knowledge, we'll share some ways to start the healing process and break the cycle.

# INTERGENERATIONAL TRAUMA EXPLAINED

So what is intergenerational trauma? Before addressing that, let's step back a bit and ask a more basic question: What is trauma?

You might think of trauma as a calamitous event, something catastrophic that happens to you. But in fact, trauma is a *response* to something bad happening. More specifically, we can define trauma as a response to an overwhelming event that causes you to fear for your life or the life and safety of someone close to you. You may have trauma because you experienced this incident directly, because you witnessed it, or because you heard vivid details from someone else (perhaps a loved one or friend). However you experience it, when an event is so overpowering that it causes a shock to the nervous system, overwhelming your ability to cope, you're experiencing trauma. A diagnosis of *post-traumatic stress disorder* (PTSD) is given to someone who has persistent, ongoing symptoms after experiencing or witnessing a traumatic event.

One of the reasons that trauma can have a long-term impact on our physical and mental health is that, often, traumatic memories are not stored the same way that our other memories are. Memories of the traumatic event might be *unintegrated*. That means that instead of residing in the past with all our other recollections, these memories can show up in the present as troubling symptoms like flashbacks, panic attacks, nightmares, anxiety, depression, and a need to avoid any reminders of the traumatic incident. They can continue to haunt us. For example, after being in a car accident, you may find your heart racing every time you approach a stoplight, or even feel panic at the thought of just getting in a car. If you had a bad experience in an earthquake, afterward you may find yourself running for cover anytime you feel a shake, even if it's just a large truck driving by.

That type of trauma is called single-incident trauma. It's produced by a onetime event that shocks the nervous system, like an accident, natural disaster, or violent attack. But trauma can also be a repeated and ongoing experience, something that occurs throughout your life, generally beginning in childhood. This is referred to as developmental or relational trauma.

The effects of developmental trauma can be more subtle than those of single-incident trauma. The cause may not be as immediately obvious as a car crash. This trauma typically comes from a parent's ongoing neglect, abuse, or misattunement (not understanding a child's needs). Because it starts in early childhood, this kind of trauma has huge ramifications for the developing brain and nervous system. To an infant whose brain is not fully developed or a child who depends fully on a caregiver, the experience can feel life-threatening. Since the trauma occurs repeatedly, it will literally shape how the brain develops, and it will therefore affect the growing child's sense of self, others, and the world into adulthood.

And this is where the concept of intergenerational trauma comes in. Intergenerational trauma is developmental trauma that is passed down through the generations. When a parent is burdened by unresolved trauma, their capacity to raise a child is impaired. Unwittingly, they inflict trauma on their children, passing the legacy on. Let's consider some examples:

Kelley experienced profound neglect as a child. Her mother had severe depression that was untreated, and she was unable to support her daughter emotionally. Her father, a traveling salesman, was rarely home. In many ways Kelley raised herself, and so she never really learned how to feel safe.

Growing up, Jeffrey was always being told by his father how he should feel. Jeffrey's father had been raised by strict and abusive parents who expected their children to be seen and not heard. Jeffrey's father and mother were never attuned to Jeffrey's feelings; in effect, he wasn't allowed to feel. As an adult, he has no connection to his own emotions and feels lost and numb in the world.

Intergenerational trauma enables a traumatic event to affect not only the person who experiences it, but also others to whom the impact is passed down through generations. This transmission can happen in several ways:

**THROUGH CAREGIVING.** As in the examples of Kelley and Jeffrey, a parent's unresolved trauma affects the way that they raise their own children.

**THROUGH GENETICS.** Trauma can also be passed through inherited traits. Studies have shown that harsh conditions can affect how certain genes function, and this alteration can be passed down to the next generation.

**THROUGH CULTURE.** Some types of intergenerational trauma are classified as "historical" or "environmental" trauma, which means they're transmitted through cultural stories, memories, living conditions, and other consequences of historic events. Much has been written about survivors of genocide, slavery, and the Holocaust, and how, generations later, impacts of that trauma affect their descendants in the form of fears and anxieties, economic disadvantage, racism, and institutionalized bias.

**AS SECONDARY TRAUMA.** As we mentioned at the beginning of the chapter, we can experience trauma secondhand by hearing about a traumatic event from someone else. In effect, our body may respond as if it happened to us. This is called secondary trauma. Children who hear vivid, repeated accounts of trauma from their parents can become traumatized themselves. Secondary trauma can even produce post-traumatic stress disorder (PTSD).

## HOW TRAUMA IS PASSED DOWN THROUGH GENERATIONS

Intergenerational trauma is pervasive in society; it occurs everywhere, across all cultures, races, and socioeconomic status. The many ways that it can be propagated have led to some "nature vs. nurture"–type debates. Some believe that nature—that is, traits and genes passed on biologically—make a person more susceptible to suffering from the effects of trauma. Those who favor the nurture side of things believe that trauma is mostly passed on through the interpersonal relationship between parents and children. It's widely accepted that both factors contribute.

**NATURE:** There's strong evidence that certain inherited traits can make someone more susceptible to developing mental health disorders such as PTSD, anxiety, depression, addiction, and other issues. However, it's important to remember that the genes we inherit don't determine our future. Our early interactions with others and the environment that we're raised in have a great impact on how the traits we inherit are shaped and expressed in our life.

**NURTURE:** When parents are attuned to their infant's cues and respond accordingly, they're supporting the development of the emotional parts of the brain and creating a predisposition for emotional well-being later in life. Conversely, a parent with unresolved trauma, with an impaired ability to manage their own emotions, may not be able to accurately read their infant's cues; they may misinterpret them or miss the cues altogether. Over time, this inadequate response to the child's needs can create impairment in the child's developing brain and nervous system.

**THE ENVIRONMENT:** The environment we grow up in is affected by historic forces such as slavery, poverty, divorce, genocide, disease, and natural disasters, with effects that can linger for generations. The impact of these kinds of events can be passed down through families in their memories and customs, and transmitted in the wider society through cultural norms and economic factors.

# EXPLORING OUR ROOTS

Does your trauma seem to be an effect of nature, nurture, environment, or a combination of the three? This exercise will help make you more conscious of the ways in which your patterns of thoughts, feelings, and behaviors come from childhood traumatic experiences. This understanding is the first step toward change.

Answer each question as best you can in the space provided.

What personality traits do you believe you inherited? List any that come to mind, positive or negative. (**Examples:** "I was born shy," "I'm a type-A personality," "I am an angry person.") For each trait you list, if you don't consider it desirable, describe how you would rather see yourself.

_____

_____

_____

_____

What are some of the norms or unspoken rules you learned growing up? (**Examples:** "Don't talk to other people," "Don't share family secrets," "Being hit and yelled at is normal.") For each norm, write down an alternative that would be healthier for you now. (**Examples:** "Secrets can be isolating, so it's better to find someone safe to share with." "It's not okay to hit or be hit.")

_____

_____

_____

_____

In what ways has history or culture affected your sense of self, others, or the world? (**Examples:** Did you grow up poor? Were your ancestors enslaved, discriminated against, or persecuted? Is your family very religious?) Considering that, how would you prefer to see yourself and others today?

_____

_____

_____

_____

_____

When you're done answering the questions, reflect on the meaning of this quote and how it relates to this exercise:

*We don't see things as they are, we see them as we are.*
—*Anaïs Nin*

After your reflection, make some notes below about what the quote means to you. How does the way you see yourself impact how you see things?

_____

_____

_____

_____

_____

# EMOTIONAL AND PHYSICAL SYMPTOMS

Intergenerational trauma can create a legacy of difficulties. One of the main effects is a decreased capacity for *self-regulation*; that is, a deficit in our ability to control our mood and how we react to emotions, sensations, and thoughts. The ability to regulate enables us to cope with stress, and it's one of the key components of good mental health. When this capability isn't working well, we can feel both physical and emotional consequences.

Our body has a built-in capacity for dealing with stress, consisting of two systems that work together to control our stress response: the sympathetic nervous system (SNS), which is responsible for arousal, and the parasympathetic nervous system (PNS), which is responsible for calming or slowing us down. You can think of managing stress like driving a car: When the gas is on (sympathetic nervous system), the car accelerates. When the brakes are on (parasympathetic nervous system), the car slows down or stops completely.

When we successfully self-regulate, we can experience emotions, sensations, and thoughts at tolerable levels. Trauma can interfere with this; it's as if the brake pedal or gas pedal gets stuck or stops working. When that happens, we find ourselves in a dysregulated state, and stress provokes one of two extremes:

**HYPERAROUSAL** is a state of being over-activated. When you are hyperaroused, you may experience shortness of breath, rapid heartbeat, anxiety, panic, fear, hypervigilance, rage, pain, hypertension, and other distressing symptoms.

**HYPOAROUSAL** is a state of being under-activated. You may experience fatigue, numbness, trouble concentrating, depression, shame, disconnection, insomnia, and dissociation (a feeling of disconnection).

We all have an optimal state between those two extremes, commonly referred to as our "window of tolerance," a term credited to Dr. Dan Siegel and illustrated by Pat Ogden, Kekuni Minton, and Claire Pain (see page 8). When we are in this window we feel at ease, able to handle the stressors of everyday life. We might get upset because we're stuck in traffic or angry that we have to work late, but it's not a crisis. We can tap the brakes or the gas a bit to slow down or speed up as needed to handle a challenge. Within the window, our nervous system is activated at a tolerable level, and we feel fine. But when stress pushes us out of the boundaries of the window, we feel the symptoms of hyper- or hypoarousal. The wider the window, the more stress you can handle without triggering a stress response.

Trauma can leave us with a very narrow window of tolerance. As a result, people who are affected by trauma may find themselves easily pushed into a state of hyperarousal or hypoarousal. When we experience stress, our nervous system hits the gas or brakes too hard, and we're pushed into a defensive mode to protect ourselves as best as we can.

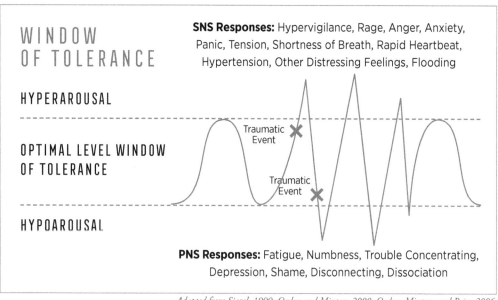

WINDOW
OF TOLERANCE

**SNS Responses:** Hypervigilance, Rage, Anger, Anxiety, Panic, Tension, Shortness of Breath, Rapid Heartbeat, Hypertension, Other Distressing Feelings, Flooding

HYPERAROUSAL

OPTIMAL LEVEL WINDOW
OF TOLERANCE

Traumatic Event

Traumatic Event

HYPOAROUSAL

**PNS Responses:** Fatigue, Numbness, Trouble Concentrating, Depression, Shame, Disconnecting, Dissociation

*Adapted from Siegel, 1999; Ogden and Minton, 2000; Ogden, Minton, and Pain, 2006.*

The reason we experience those symptoms is because of our physical reaction to a perceived threat. It's a reflex similar to that found in other animals: When we're in danger we have an instinct to fight, flee, or freeze. If the sympathetic nervous system becomes active, your heart beats faster, blood flows to your extremities (which is why your face feels warm when you're stressed), and you breathe faster to bring oxygen to your muscles. These reactions prepare your body to fight or to run away. If you can't do either, a freeze response can be triggered. The parasympathetic system kicks in, and you may faint, start feeling numb, have a sensation of being outside of your body, or experience dissociation—a state of shutting down so completely that there's a break or disconnection between mind, thoughts, feelings, and sensations. This kind of response is seen in sexual assault, when a person wants to run but is unable to escape or take other action.

All too often, people suffering from intergenerational trauma have a narrow window of tolerance without realizing why and suffer when stress pushes them above or below the window. Along with the physical symptoms mentioned above, emotional symptoms can result: anxiety and depression, loneliness, withdrawal, isolation, numbing, grief, fear, sadness, anger, and shame. Prolonged time spent outside the window of tolerance takes a toll on physical health and can lead to chronic health issues including autoimmune disorders, gastrointestinal disorders, cardiovascular issues, memory loss, sleep disturbances, weight issues, and addiction issues. These symptoms affect us not only emotionally and physically, but also in terms of our sense of self, safety, and the way we relate to others.

# INVENTORY OF EMOTIONAL AND PHYSICAL SYMPTOMS

This exercise will help you identify some of the physical and emotional symptoms that are typically associated with trauma. Often, people with trauma are cut off from noticing how their body and mind respond to stress because they've become accustomed to the symptoms. Or they're hyper-focused on their responses, without connecting them to the roots of their trauma. This exercise will help you better recognize symptoms that may be related to your trauma.

Please circle the symptoms that you are aware of, and feel free to write in additional ones that apply to you:

|  | PHYSICAL | EMOTIONAL |
|---|---|---|
| **HYPERAROUSAL** | Shortness of breath | Anxiety |
| | Rapid heartbeat | Panic |
| | Nightmares | Fear |
| | Heightened startle response | Freezing |
| | Sleep issues | Irritability |
| | Addiction | Agitation |
| | Chronic pain | Anger |
| | Panic attacks | Rage |
| | Attention difficulties | Confusion |
| | Agitation | Fearfulness |
| | GI problems | Overwhelm |
| | Hypertension | Hypervigilance |
| | Elevated blood pressure | Mistrust |
| | Bingeing | Impulsivity |
| | Purging | Shame |
| | Headaches | Depression |
| | Intrusive imagery | Loneliness |
| | Environmental sensitivity | Withdrawal |

*Table continues* ⟶

|  | PHYSICAL | EMOTIONAL |
|---|---|---|
| **HYPOAROUSAL** | Fatigue | Isolation |
|  | Insomnia | Derealization |
|  | Fogginess | Shutdown |
|  | Numbness | Numbness |
|  | Memory Loss | Dissociation |
|  | Addiction | Grief |
|  | Restricting | Sadness |
|  | Fibromyalgia | Guilt |
|  | Chronic fatigue syndrome | Hopelessness |
|  | Lethargy | Helplessness |
|  | Confusion | Worthlessness |
|  |  | Deadness |

After you've identified some of your personal symptoms, take a few moments to appreciate the beginning of your healing journey. Sit comfortably in a relaxed place and begin to notice your breathing. Feel the sensations of your breath, and repeat this phrase three times, out loud or in your mind:

*My symptoms are the gateway to understanding and healing.*

As you say these words and take these breaths, see if you can allow yourself to feel hope. It's okay if you can't. Just try to notice how you feel, without judgment. And know that you're taking powerful healing steps.

Sit comfortably and reflect on this for as long as you like.

# IMPACT ON LIFE AND RELATIONSHIPS

Physical and emotional symptoms are not the only ways intergenerational trauma impacts our lives. Trauma also impacts our sense of self, our relationships with others, and our sense of safety.

As we've discussed, all infants are dependent on their primary caregivers to survive and thrive. From the beginning, the infant's brain and nervous system are shaped by interactions between the primary caregiver and child. These early interactions set up the way this child will see themselves and relationships throughout life. With good enough attunement (no parent is perfect), a child will feel safe, loved, and good enough in the world. But if the caregiver has unresolved trauma, their ability to attune—to understand the child's signals for being held, fed, changed, and soothed—may be compromised. The child that's not soothed by their parent may not only feel unsafe, but may also very likely develop a poor sense of self; that is, an unstable sense of identity and self-worth, not knowing who they really are or what they want, need, or believe.

When Mary was born, her father had recently died, so she was raised by a grieving parent. Her mother's reduced capacity left Mary feeling unsafe in the world, never knowing what to expect. When Mary gave birth to her own daughter, Bethany, she was overwrought with anxiety about keeping her daughter safe. She constantly misread Bethany's cues and became extremely overprotective, sometimes even waking the baby up and never letting her child leave her sight.

A child raised by a parent with an inability to soothe may develop deficits in their ability to self-regulate and develop other strategies in order to survive. For example, a child who's not comforted often enough when they cry will protest at first, then simply stop crying. In effect, this child internalizes that no one will come when they cry. As they grow, the child might develop a sense of shame for having needs, and a deep-seated anger that continues into adulthood.

Someone who grows up with an inner sense of being bad or unlovable will have difficulty forming intimate relationships. The dilemma of wanting closeness but also being afraid of it because of early painful relationships makes it hard to form healthy attachments. That person's legacy of trauma informs all their relationships, and as a parent they may unknowingly repeat this pattern with their own children. In this way, unresolved intergenerational trauma can be passed not only from one person to their child, but also further down through the generations.

As we explore the impact of intergenerational trauma on our lives and relationships, you'll find it helpful to look more deeply at yourself. Identifying positive and negative thoughts and beliefs is the first step in uncovering ways that trauma has impacted your life. In the table opposite, we have provided some of the core issues that we find in those with trauma; you can use these or add some of your own.

Please circle the statements below that best describe you.

To continue this exercise, when you hear yourself making one of the negative statements from the left column, try replacing it by making the corresponding positive statement from the right column.

Try reading the positive statements aloud. How do you feel when you say them? What sensations, emotions, and images come up when you focus on the positive statements?

_____

_____

_____

_____

The statements in the right column of the previous table can be used as positive affirmations. Write a list of the ones that feel most applicable to you, and post them on your mirror or some other spot where you'll see them every day. Say them out loud when you see them, even if they don't fit your current mood.

Make up some of your own affirmations to add to the list. Write them below.

_____

_____

_____

_____

| | |
|---|---|
| It's not easy for me to form relationships. | It's easy for me to form relationships. |
| I don't expect others to treat me well. | I trust that I will be treated well by others. |
| I find it difficult to connect with or know my own needs. | It's easy for me to identify what I want and need for myself. |
| I don't know what I want from relationships. | I know what I want from other people. |
| I never quite feel safe with my intimate partners. | I feel safe with intimate relationships. |
| I feel ashamed when I need something. | I'm comfortable with having needs. |
| I feel uncomfortable asking people for help, or I won't ask for help. | It's easy for me to ask others for help. |
| I often put others' needs ahead of my own. | I feel good about allowing myself time for self-care. |
| I criticize myself for mistakes and expect perfection. | I allow myself to make mistakes with compassion. |
| I secretly feel that if people get to know me too well, they may reject me. | I expect that when people get to know me, they will like me. |
| I don't often find it necessary to share feelings with others. | I find comfort in sharing my feelings, whether they're negative or positive. |
| I don't find a need for friendships. | I like having friends. |
| I find the world to be a scary place, or I'm always waiting for the other shoe to drop. | Generally I feel safe in the world. |
| I have a sense that something is wrong with me. | I feel comfortable in my own skin. |
| I don't deserve good things. | I deserve good things. |
| I find it hard to love myself. | I have self-love. |

# TREATING INTERGENERATIONAL TRAUMA

Trauma's effects on brain development are long-lasting. But there is good news: Our brains are changeable.

The nerve cell connections in our brain, called neural pathways, communicate with each other to determine our perceptions, senses, habits, and behaviors. The effect of trauma on how these pathways form, especially at a young age, results in many of the symptoms we've been discussing. But it turns out that our brains can create new neural pathways all throughout our lives. Over time, new experiences and repeating new healthier habits can rewire our brain to enable a healthy sense of self. As new connections form in our brain, we develop a capacity for healthier relationships and new ways of being in the world.

As mentioned in the introduction to this book, the help of a therapist is crucial for anyone who's experiencing symptoms of unresolved trauma. One of the most healing aspects of therapy, whatever type, is the relationship between the therapist and the client. The therapeutic relationship provides an opportunity to develop and strengthen regulation skills that have been affected by trauma, in a nonjudgmental atmosphere.

There are many types, or modalities, of therapy available to help with intergenerational trauma. Whichever type of therapy you pursue—you'll find information about choosing a therapist in the last chapter of this book—we recommend that it include these elements:

**A COLLABORATIVE, NONJUDGMENTAL APPROACH.** As mentioned, we find that this style provides a safe place for healing.

**AN INITIAL FOCUS ON STABILIZATION.** We believe that it's very important for therapy to begin with stabilization and symptom reduction. Stabilization means helping you feel safe and learn not to be overwhelmed by your feelings or sensations.

**A MEASURED PACE.** To start, it's important to take things slow and build up the skills needed for emotional and physical regulation. The therapist should help the client slowly build their ability to tolerate distress, gradually expanding their window of tolerance. Diving into painful trauma memories should only be done after this first phase has been completed. After processing traumatic memories, therapy should continue to integrate new skills and help you imagine a future based on new abilities to connect, a new sense of safety, and a new sense of self.

Let's take a look at some of the therapies most commonly used for treating trauma. The exercises in this book draw from these various modalities, or types of therapy.

**COGNITIVE BEHAVIORAL THERAPY (CBT)** is based on the premise that our thoughts, emotions, and behaviors are all connected and influence each other, which means that changing one will affect the others. CBT focuses on the present and on solving current problems. The therapy explores core beliefs and provides methods to help identify, examine, and shift *cognitive distortions*: negative, irrational beliefs. Intergenerational trauma can cause these unhealthy beliefs to be passed down from one generation to the next. CBT helps people identify and challenge cognitive distortions and experiment with new and healthier behaviors. We'll take a closer look at cognitive distortions in chapter 3.

**COGNITIVE PROCESSING THERAPY (CPT)** focuses more on how we process distress, emphasizing self-awareness as a component of change. This type of therapy is often time-limited and focuses on the past trauma, not the present moment. The goal is to help people understand their trauma so they can reduce the habit of avoiding their thoughts and feelings. CPT therapists particularly focus on safety, trust, power, control, esteem, and intimacy to create healthier functioning. For example, David, coming into therapy for PTSD after returning from military service in Afghanistan, will be taught about PTSD symptoms and then asked to describe his symptoms, going all the way back to trauma experienced in his childhood. The therapist will work with David, using his memories, thoughts, and beliefs to help him regulate his feelings and modify cognitive distortions.

**DIALECTICAL BEHAVIOR THERAPY (DBT)** emphasizes emotional regulation, distress tolerance, mindfulness (more about this shortly), and interpersonal effectiveness. Considered a form of CBT therapy, DBT relies on building new skills, teaching people how to live in the moment, and using acceptance and understanding to let go of rigid, black-and-white thinking.

**EYE MOVEMENT DESENSITIZATION REPROCESSING (EMDR)** therapy focuses on trauma that hasn't been fully processed, and thus is held differently from other memories—unintegrated memories, as we described earlier in this chapter. The idea is to reprocess those memories and integrate them in a healthier way. EMDR uses the technique of bilateral stimulation—alternately stimulating the left and right hemispheres of the brain through eye movement, tapping, or other stimuli. Accessing both sides of the brain helps integrate the memories and create new neural pathways.

**MINDFULNESS** is the art of learning to bring your attention to the present moment, without judgment. Mindfulness skills are used with other therapies to help people notice and accept feelings, sensations, and thoughts as they happen. Trauma can make us feel hijacked by the past; mindfulness helps by returning us to the present. Mindfulness can also help clients become more aware of physical sensations; both discomfort relating to trauma, and feelings of calm and comfort.

**SOMATIC THERAPIES,** including somatic experiencing (SE), sensorimotor psychotherapy (SP), trauma resiliency model (TRM), neuroaffective relational model (NARM), and neuroaffective touch (NT), focus on the mind-body connection. By bringing attention to the sensations, movements, and/or posture, the therapist can gently explore how the body has been affected by unresolved trauma. Suppressed emotions become evident and can be processed in a gentle way.

# IT CAN STOP WITH YOU

Learning about trauma that may have originated decades ago and may have been passed down unwittingly by your own family can make you feel as if the problem is beyond your control. You may be wondering if you are predestined to repeat the cycle and continue the unconscious behaviors, patterns, and feelings that have been passed on to you through the generations. It's only natural to wonder about that, but the evidence is conclusive: No matter how deeply rooted your intergenerational trauma may be, you can begin the steps to break the cycle.

Understanding intergenerational trauma and recognizing how it has affected your life can feel overwhelming, but they are important and necessary first steps. Only by uncovering patterns that have been passed down can we begin to interrupt them. Realizing that much of our behavior and emotions have deep roots in our earliest interactions can help us better understand why we are the way we are. Then, we can take action and replace the unhealthy effects of trauma with new thoughts and behaviors, rewiring our brains for a healthy future.

# Lydia

Lydia sought therapy because she was struggling with feeling like she was not a good enough parent. She described always having a fear that she "wasn't enough" and that there wasn't going to be enough to go around. This applied to everything: She feared there wouldn't be enough money, enough food, enough connection to her children. It became evident through therapy that these fears contributed to her becoming a controlling parent. Lydia hovered obsessively over her children, and she rarely splurged on extra clothes, entertainment, or anything that wasn't a necessity.

Lydia's mother and father were children during the Great Depression and had shared stories with her of what their life was like then. Her parents lived their entire lives as though the Depression was still happening or could imminently happen again. Lydia's parents felt this threat throughout their childhood, and then as parents themselves continued to convey a fear of deprivation—which Lydia then developed and was now passing on to her own children. Lydia's cupboard was overflowing with canned goods in case of emergency, and her children hid food in their rooms. The challenge was for Lydia to overcome living with fear and a sense of scarcity.

Lydia was able to integrate her past trauma by experiencing how her present beliefs and emotions were directly linked to the trauma of her parents and grandparents. This enabled her to recognize that these feelings really belong in the past. Grounding herself in the present moment, Lydia increased her capacity to be aware of the safety and stability of her present-day life. Learning to practice this mindfulness in her own parenting improved Lydia's relationships with her children, since she could now parent from a more regulated state.

# BEGINNING MY JOURNEY

This exercise will help you solidify some important points that you've learned in this chapter and help set goals for your self-exploration going forward.

In the space below, journal about the impact intergenerational trauma has had on your life and how you would like to change. Take as long as you like to record your thoughts. Here are some writing prompts that may be helpful.

- Look back at the exercise Exploring Our Roots (page 5) for ideas of how nature, nurture, or environment has affected your sense of self, others, or the world.

- Look back at your Inventory of Physical and Emotional Symptoms (page 9) and consider how your physical and emotional symptoms are affecting you, your relationships, and your understanding of the world.

- Review your answers in Uncovering Core Issues (page 12), and journal about your sense of the effects of those beliefs on you, your relationships, and your view of the world.

When you're finished writing, take a moment for reflection. Sit comfortably and breathe naturally, feeling the sensations of your breath. Notice the feeling of your feet on the ground, your body on the seat, your spine against the back of the chair. Then, try to imagine how you'd feel if you didn't have the difficulties connected to your trauma. If that's difficult or impossible to imagine, don't be discouraged. You are not alone, and your healing journey is just beginning.

# CHAPTER HIGHLIGHTS

- Trauma is a response to an overwhelming event that causes you to fear for your life or the life and safety of someone close to you.

- Intergenerational trauma occurs when the effects of trauma are passed down from one generation to another. This affects our sense of self, others, and the world.

- Effects of intergenerational trauma begin in early childhood and can continue to affect us throughout life.

- Intergenerational trauma can be transmitted via inherited traits (nature), family relationships and customs (nurture), environmental conditions (culture and memories), or a combination of these factors.

- Our brains are capable of change throughout life, enabling us to heal and recover from intergenerational trauma.

- Understanding and exploring the roots of trauma symptoms are the first steps toward change.

- Trauma therapy is best practiced with stabilization and establishment of safety being the first priorities.

# CHAPTER 2

# EXPLORING THE PAST

Perhaps you already have some sense of the far-reaching effect that intergenerational trauma has on your life. Or maybe you've only just begun exploring how your family's history is impacting you. Either way, considering your past from a new perspective will help you develop insights into your present-day problems and the ways that you can find solutions.

In this chapter, we'll begin to explore how the past influences our lives in the here and now. The exercises in these pages aren't about blame or judgment; they're meant to help you more fully understand your roots and learn how to untangle the past from the present. This chapter will also provide tools to help you develop self-compassion and resources to help you return to your window of tolerance when life pushes you out of your comfort zone.

# IMPORTANCE OF EXPLORATION

Whatever circumstances we were raised in, we're all influenced by patterns of behavior that have been passed down to us through our caregivers, our families, and our culture. These influences color our way of seeing and experiencing ourselves, others, and the world. These patterns affect how, from a very young age, we make meaning out of physical sensations and emotions. When these patterns are skewed by intergenerational trauma, they can be at the root of many mental, psychological, and physical problems. Understanding these patterns, and how they resulted in depression, anxiety, addiction, physical distress, and other health issues, is the first step in breaking the intergenerational trauma cycle. When you heal your own trauma, you avoid passing it along to another generation.

This part of your journey may at times bring up difficult emotions, so we invite you to try to undertake this process without judgment toward yourself. Keep in mind the familiar quote: "Those who cannot remember the past are condemned to repeat it." The goal in understanding your family's trauma, how it affected them, how it affected you growing up, and how it continues to affect you today isn't to assign blame to you or anyone else. Rather, you're learning to understand yourself from a new perspective so you can follow a different path.

# WHAT MAY BLOCK YOUR EXPLORATION

It may be difficult to look at your family history in a new way. You may feel at times that you're criticizing or judging the family that you love. You may feel extremely angry as you explore painful aspects of your family's past. You may find deeply rooted conflicts within yourself; you might be proud of your family heritage and feel uncomfortable about challenging it. Or you might have a sense of shame or sadness about your family's past, and not want to examine it.

It's not always easy to explore our family history. Sometimes families don't talk about their past; sometimes there are family secrets. You may not remember much about your own childhood. Trauma survivors often have missing pieces of the past, especially when childhood experiences are too traumatic to be processed correctly into memory or when they happen preverbally. In some cases, children protect themselves by dissociation—that is, by disconnecting from the moment so completely that no memories are left. In some cases, the experience may be expressed through physical sensations that profoundly influence us—headaches, anxiety, or an ongoing sense of being uncomfortable in the world.

For some people who've lived through traumatic experiences, it can be as if a Pandora's box that's deep inside of them holds aspects of their past that they are unable to deal with. When you begin to explore or open that box, it's important to open it slowly and with support. Healing intergenerational trauma is a marathon, not a sprint.

As you begin your journey of exploration, it's important to start from a calm place. This first exercise can be a valuable resource in helping you prepare for your journey.

# CALM PLACE MINDFULNESS

This exercise, taken from somatic therapies, will help you cope with unregulated emotions by empowering you to return to a place of calm and peace. Use it when you find yourself feeling stressed and outside of your window of tolerance.

This calm place can be somewhere you've been, somewhere you've seen in a photograph, painting, or movie, or somewhere you've read about in a book. It can be a specific memory of a time or a moment that was calm and relaxing, like baking cookies with Grandma, or an imagined image, like watching a beautiful sunset or sunrise.

1. Find a comfortable sitting position in a quiet place where you won't be disturbed. You can close your eyes for this exercise or focus your sight on one spot in the room.

2. Ground yourself by noticing the feelings of your feet on the ground, your body on the seat, your back against the chair or sofa.

3. Begin to notice your sensations of breathing. Without trying to change or control your breathing pattern, simply feel the air moving in and out of your lungs and your chest rising and falling. If your mind wanders during the exercise, that's okay. Gently bring your attention back to your breathing and continue.

4. Try to relax any areas of your body where you feel stress or tension.

5. Now, bring into your mind's eye a place that is peaceful, calm, or happy. Somewhere real or imagined that makes you smile.

6. Imagine this place using all your senses. What colors, shapes, and movements do you see? What are the sounds and smells? What might you touch? What's the temperature, and what does the air feel like?

7. As you keep imagining the scene, notice the emotions that come along with the sensations.

8. Take some slow, deep breaths as you hang out in your calm place. Remain there as long as you like. When you're ready, take some slow, deep breaths and gently bring your attention back to your surroundings.

After trying this exercise for the first time, take a moment to reflect. What shift in your emotions did you notice? Were you able to experience calmness, peacefulness, or happiness? If not, try not to judge yourself; practice again when you're ready. It might be helpful to look at a photograph or image to bring your imagination to a calm place.

Try practicing this skill when you're feeling within your window of tolerance, so you'll be able to call on it more easily when you need it most.

# UNLOCKING THE PAST

Intergenerational trauma often goes unrecognized or may be misdiagnosed as another mental health condition. When some people seek help for depression, anxiety, obsessive-compulsive disorder, or addiction, the connection between these issues and the impact of the past can go unnoticed. *Trauma-informed therapy* views most symptoms as having an origin in traumatic roots. A therapist who's aware of the effects of trauma on the brain, nervous system, and a person's cognitive and emotional systems can see past the symptoms and get to the roots.

Bridget was seeking treatment because of her pattern of entering into abusive relationships. When asked if there were problems in her family history, Bridget replied, "No, it was fine, nothing bothered me, it was just the way it was." In truth, she had grown up in a home with violence, addiction, and mental illness, but to her this was normal. Bridget's father struggled with substance abuse, and her mother suffered from depression. Bridget never realized the impact her parents' difficulties had on her, and she didn't realize that in order to survive and function, she had learned to numb herself, either with drugs or by dissociating from her feelings. Although Bridget suffered from depression throughout her life, she didn't connect this to her childhood family trauma until well into her 40s, when she began her intergenerational trauma therapy. Bridget was the first person in her family to begin therapy and healing, thus breaking the chain of unspoken trauma that had been passed down not only from her parents, but also from her grandparents before them.

Typically in stories like Bridget's, people seek therapy and are treated for symptoms such as depression or anxiety, but they may not find relief—or their symptoms may go away for a time only to return in some other form. Often after repeated failures, a client may begin to read or hear about intergenerational trauma or be referred to trauma-informed therapy. Others begin therapy for problems in relationships or because they feel dissatisfied, stuck, or unfulfilled.

However you came to the concept of intergenerational trauma, it's important to realize that the roots of your trauma are deep and may have begun before you were born.

# Albert

Albert, an African American man in his 30s, came into treatment feeling he could never get ahead and the world was against him. He was an only child raised by a single mother; he knew little about his father, except that he had abandoned them when Albert was one. Albert felt like he was a mistake, that he never belonged. He talked about what a wonderful mother he had growing up, although, because she worked long hours, he spent a lot of time at neighbors' homes. His mother came home exhausted, and he felt he had to take care of her, not cause any trouble or ask for too much of her attention.

Albert's mother believed that you had to fight to get ahead. She often spoke about the prejudice she'd faced on a daily basis while growing up in the South and living through segregation. She taught Albert that being African American meant that he was always in danger. She once told him to never run in public, because people would assume he'd done something wrong and he might get himself shot. Albert had a sense that people feared him because he was a large man, and he never felt welcome anywhere. At the start of therapy Albert could not make eye contact with the therapist. He learned that this was a sign of shame, feeling not good enough, and fearing he would be judged and hated. Over time, Albert came to understand how his beliefs became self-sabotaging: He expected others to reject him, so he rejected them first and ended up always feeling desperately lonely. Though Albert received many social invitations, he typically found reasons to decline, feeling that he really wasn't wanted.

Through therapy, Albert became able to take more risks, not always fearing he would be rejected or judged. He began to change his pattern of rejecting others and started to make more social plans. The work was slow but steady, and Albert was able to feel safer in the world and find meaningful connections with others.

This exercise is designed to help you identify the roots of intergenerational trauma by diagramming patterns of trauma that have occurred in your family history through several generations. This genogram, or map of family history, can reveal patterns that might have been previously unexamined and hidden. Becoming aware of patterns and issues that were passed down through family or culture will help you make changes in your life.

Start by reviewing the sample genogram below. In this example, Albert included a sixth-generation tier because of the impact of slavery on his family. Follow the model to create your own, including at least three generations if you can.

## SAMPLE GENOGRAM

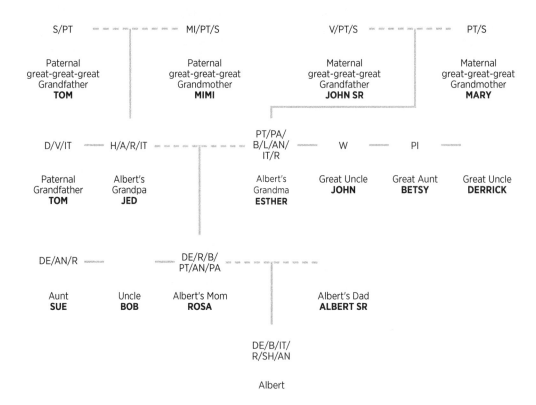

This sample genogram shows the story of Albert's family (see sidebar on page 27). The descriptors indicate that Albert experienced depression (DE), anxiety (AN), bullying (B), racism (R), shame (SH), and intergenerational trauma (IT). Albert knows nothing about his father, so his father's square is blank. Albert believes that his mother, Rosa, suffered from depression (DE), racism (R), bullying (B), physical abuse (PA), PTSD (PT), and anxiety (AN). Rosa is connected to Albert's Aunt Sue, whom Albert recalled as being depressed (DE), anxious (AN), and experiencing racism (R), and to his deceased Uncle Bob, whom Albert knows nothing about.

At the top of the genogram are Albert's great-great-great grandparents, who lived as slaves (S). Though Albert only knows tidbits, he assumes that each suffered PTSD. Albert knew the most about his maternal grandparents, though they died before he was born. His grandfather struggled with alcohol abuse and often became violent, and his grandmother was loving to his mother, but she was also physically abused by her husband and likely suffered with PTSD, along with anxiety, racism, and bullying. She was not able to protect her daughter, Albert's mother, from Grandpa Jed's violence. After completing his genogram, Albert saw more clearly the effect of each generation on the other, and the roots of his depression, anxiety, and sense of shame. He also saw how he carried the intergenerational trauma of slavery.

1. Use the space on page 31 to create your own genogram, or use a separate sheet of paper if you want more room. You can also create your genogram with a digital drawing app of your choice.

2. Begin by drawing a symbol representing yourself near the bottom of the page (see the symbol list on page 31).

3. If you have siblings, add their symbols in line with yours, and connect them to your symbol with a horizontal line.

4. Add descriptors from the list on page 31 to reflect the circumstances affecting you and your siblings.

5. Extend a vertical line upward from your symbol, connecting to symbols representing your parents. Draw horizontal lines to connect your parents and their siblings.

6. Write in the descriptors for your parents and their siblings.

7. Repeat through the generations as far back as you can go.

Here are some common descriptors:

A: addiction

AD: attention-deficit hyperactivity disorder (ADHD)

ADP: adoption

AN: anxiety

B: bullying

DE: depression

DIS: disability

D: divorce

G: genocide/Holocaust

H: hostility

IT: intergenerational trauma

L: loving

MI: mental illness

NC: national crisis (e.g., an economic depression)

ND: natural disaster (e.g., a famine or earthquake)

O: obsessive-compulsive disorder (OCD)

PA: physical abuse

PI: physical illness

P: poverty

PT: PTSD

R: racism

SA: sexual abuse

SH: shame

S: slavery

SU: suicide

V: violence

W: war

Add your own descriptors here if you don't see them listed:

_____

_____

_____

_____

## GENOGRAM SYMBOLS:

☐  MALE

○  FEMALE

△  NON-BINARY

X  DECEASED

- - - -  DIVORCED OR ESTRANGED

———  TOGETHER/MARRIED

Use this space for your genogram.

After completing your genogram, you can visualize how each family member's history may have affected other family members, the next generation, and all the way down to you and your current family branch.

What patterns do you see? For example, do you see patterns of chronic racism, poverty, anger, depression, early death, abuse, or mental illness?

_____

_____

_____

_____

_____

What do you notice in your life today that may have come from these patterns?

_____

_____

_____

_____

_____

Are there current family members who you just now realize might be toxic or abusive?

_____

_____

_____

_____

_____

Are there historical or cultural influences?

_____

_____

_____

_____

Thinking about your family history may bring up a lot. It can stir up feelings of shame, anger, despair, and other unpleasant feelings. When we begin to look into our past, we don't always like what we see there. So how do you move forward? We have found that practicing self-care is a wonderful way to ease the troubled heart. In this sense, we mean self-care as a healthy practice of something that helps you expand positive feelings (we'll talk more about this in chapter 5). For example, you can take a walk, pamper yourself, listen to music, meditate, or call a friend. We've also found that positive statements (affirmations) can be very helpful. Repeat the following affirmation out loud, and then write in some self-care activities you can practice today.

> *When I reflect on my family history, I realize I am not my past. The family past does not define me. I can choose new paths. I can break the chains of intergenerational trauma. I will practice self-care by doing something kind for myself today.*

Write below three self-care activities for today:

1. _____

2. _____

3. _____

# THE UNWANTED GIFTS

Now that you're thinking about your family tree, do you see things passed down that you would rather not have received? We cannot control what unwanted gifts are given to us, but we do have the ability to grow and change what we do with those gifts. In this exercise, try writing about what came up for you when you were working on your genogram, following the prompts below.

Write about your emotional and physical responses, such as sadness, anger, shame, or physical sensations of distress. Write about what the process was like, and what you learned from it.

_____

_____

_____

_____

_____

Did you gain any new understandings of your family story?

Write about any patterns that you are now seeing; describe them. List some descriptors that you may share with others in your family.

_____

_____

_____

_____

_____

What have you learned about your family? What you have learned about love in your family? What have you have learned about the transmission of intergenerational trauma?

_____

_____

_____

_____

_____

_____

_____

_____

_____

_____

Working on your genogram may have brought up sadness, anger, confusion, or other uncomfortable feelings. Recognize that these feelings are normal, and give yourself permission to acknowledge that looking at your family patterns can be difficult. Remember that it's okay to feel negative feelings. If your emotions become too big at any point, you can orient yourself to the present moment and leave your history behind with this exercise:

1. Sit comfortably and bring your attention to the present moment. Notice your breathing; feel your body in the chair and your feet on the ground.

2. Turn your head to the left. Notice and name something that you see, either out loud or In your head.

3. Turn your head to the right, and name something that you see.

4. Remind yourself that the past is not happening now; in this moment, you are safe.

5. Slowly return your awareness to your surroundings.

# UNDERSTANDING THE ROOTS OF YOUR TRAUMA

As we unlock the past, we have an opportunity to understand the roots and the origins of intergenerational trauma. This is an important step. Getting to a place of understanding isn't always easy. It may take some time to uncover stories, information, or memories that you had forgotten about or never knew. You may only remember bits and pieces at a time as you are ready for them.

Bethany had felt the pain of depression since middle school. She had used cutting and alcohol to help numb her painful feelings. When she created a genogram as a project in a college art class, she asked her mother about their family history. Bethany was amazed to find out that her grandmother had committed suicide, and that her great-grandmother was known to have had depression, as did her mother. Learning that her own depression was partly inherited offered some relief for Bethany, who began to understand why her mother was depressed and to have compassion rather than anger for her mother. Bethany was able to start healing by practicing nurturing and self-care, giving herself some of the nurturing she missed out on as a child.

Sometimes families have secrets; if you ask family members for family stories, they may shut down, get suspicious, or feel that you are going to blame them for your problems. They may not volunteer information. Here are some ideas to help you if your family is resistant.

**START WITH YOUR ALLIES.** If there are family members whom you're not comfortable speaking with, ask "safe" relatives for their memories. You may find enough useful information without needing to approach more problematic sources.

**STICK TO FACT-FINDING.** Your relatives don't need to know your private reasons for seeking information about your family history. You can simply say that you want to know more about your roots and your heritage.

**RETURN TO A CALM PLACE.** When your exploration becomes frustrating, manage your stress levels with a meditation like the Calm Place Mindfulness exercise on page 24.

**WORK WITH WHAT YOU HAVE.** Even if you end up not learning much about your family history, you can still heal and grow. You can use your own present-day descriptors to imagine the history that came before. The very act of investigating the past is a way of acknowledging that you're not to blame for influences beyond your control.

# YOUR FAMILY STORY

This exercise will help deepen your understanding of the full impact that intergenerational trauma has had on each generation of your family. This knowledge can help you understand your symptoms in a different way.

Use the prompts below to write about each generation of your family, and how you imagine the trauma that you've identified may have impacted their lives. If you didn't know your great grandparents or grandparents, write about what you know about them from stories you have heard. If there have been other important primary caretakers or influential presences in your life—stepparents, aunts, uncles, close family friends—please include them as well.

Contemplating what you know about your family roots, write about the trauma of your great-grandparents, and how it affected your grandparents.

---------------------------------------------------

---------------------------------------------------

---------------------------------------------------

---------------------------------------------------

---------------------------------------------------

Write about the trauma of your grandparents, and how it affected your parents.

---------------------------------------------------

---------------------------------------------------

---------------------------------------------------

---------------------------------------------------

Write about the trauma of your parents, and how it affected you growing up.

_____

_____

_____

_____

_____

How does your family's trauma affect you presently, in terms of how you think about yourself?

_____

_____

_____

_____

_____

How does the trauma affect your existing relationships?

_____

_____

_____

_____

_____

How does the trauma affect you presently, in terms of your sense of safety in the world?

_____

_____

_____

_____

_____

_____

After imagining and writing about your family roots, it's helpful to reflect. This can deepen your sense of connection and understanding between past and present. At the same time, it can help you let go of what is in the past and redefine your present self.

To prepare for reflection on what you've learned about your family, sit comfortably and come into connection with your breath. Then, say this affirmation to yourself (out loud or in your mind):

> *When I reflect on my family patterns, I realize I am not to blame. There was something wrong with my environment; this is not an indictment of me. Now that I have uncovered the roots of my difficulties, I can break the cycle.*

Even if you don't know that much about your family—perhaps there's no one to ask, or no one who will share—you can remind yourself that patterns were created before your time; there are patterns you inherited, passed down to you through the generations. This awareness is enough for you to start anew in the present and open up to new connections and possibilities.

# BREATHING TO RELEASE TENSION

Slowing down and deepening our breath can help bring us into the current moment to feel calm and relaxed. This is a strategy you can use anytime, anywhere, when you begin to feel out of sorts, anxious, upset, or stressed. Sometimes people hold their breath when they are out of their window of tolerance, so remembering to breathe is a first step in self-soothing and learning to calm yourself.

1.  Sitting or standing, place your hands behind your head with your fingers interlocking. You can close your eyes for this exercise or keep them open.

2.  Take slow, deep breaths, breathing in through your nose and out through your mouth. Allow the breath to move down to your belly as you inhale. Notice your belly rising with each inhalation and deflating with each exhalation.

3.  You can rest your hands on your thighs or on the arms of your chair as you continue, or keep them behind your head, whichever you prefer.

4.  As you continue awareness of your breathing, notice how your breath deepens. Invite your shoulders to relax. See if you can notice tension in your jaw; allow your jaw to relax. Continue to relax any areas of tension as you breathe: Imagine your jaw, your forehead, your eyes, your shoulders, your chest, your belly, and your core relaxing.

5.  Imagine golden strands from above gently pulling you upward and elongating your spine; notice how your breath deepens as your spine stretches.

6.  Now, notice what you're feeling and experiencing. Continue breathing deeply until you begin to feel calmer, or until you're ready to end the exercise. When you're finished, gently return your attention to your surroundings.

The next step is to make this exercise a part of your daily routine. It may take some practice for your body to learn to relax, so keep at it. Practice when you're upset, but also practice at times when you're not stressed. The more you practice, the more easily you will remember to use your breath as a calming tool.

## NOTES

- It may be tricky, at first, to regulate in-breaths and out-breaths, to avoid hyperventilating or getting dizzy. If you have problems at any point, adjust by breathing less deeply and allowing your natural flow of breath to assert itself.

- If you find deep breathing distressing, as an alternative sensory exercise, try listening to some calming music and focus on the sounds of the music, and/or light some scented candles or incense that appeals to your sense of smell. Simply sit comfortably and take in the sound and aroma, not changing your breathing, just experiencing your senses.

# CHAPTER HIGHLIGHTS

- Intergenerational trauma can skew how we understand our physical and emotional symptoms, often leading to misdiagnoses.

- Understanding the roots of present symptoms facilitates healing trauma and allows something new to take its place.

- A genogram, or family tree, is a valuable tool to help visualize and understand the symptoms and patterns that run through the generations.

- Untangling the roots of your intergenerational trauma will help you uncouple the past from the present.

- Understanding the way trauma is passed down to you will be helpful in developing a nonjudgmental attitude toward yourself.

- Using tools to help you self-soothe and adopt nonjudgmental attitudes toward yourself and others will help you expand your window of tolerance and sense of ease.

# CHAPTER 3

# UNDERSTANDING YOUR BELIEFS

In this chapter we're going to focus on how intergenerational trauma affects the development of our belief system—the conscious and unconscious core beliefs that powerfully shape how we think, feel, act, and interact. We'll start with the roots of distorted thinking, how our distorted thoughts are maintained and become automatic, and how they can be challenged and changed.

# BELIEFS AND DISTORTED THINKING

We're not always aware of what we are thinking, or how much our thinking influences the way that we feel. Especially prone to going unnoticed are *automatic thoughts*—those thoughts that pop into our consciousness seemingly of their own accord and repeat so frequently that we stop being aware of them. For many of us, these automatic thoughts are negative and have a significant and detrimental impact on how we judge ourselves and our relationships.

Paula always thought she wasn't very smart. Growing up, her mother was always quick to help Paula, never letting her do anything for herself. As an adult, Paula worked in a job she hated, but she believed that she wasn't able to learn to do anything else. Her automatic thoughts include: *I'm so stupid. I can never get ahead. I will always have to depend on someone smarter than me to get through life.*

Where do these kinds of thoughts come from? Our thoughts have origins in our personal history and beliefs. Elements of our earliest environment—including relationships with our family, socioeconomic status, cultural norms, and events of the world—all contribute to create a set of core beliefs through which we see ourselves and others.

These deeply held beliefs influence how we interpret our experience. Much of our behaviors, attitudes, and ways of being in the world are based on our core beliefs. Your core beliefs color your perception of the world. It's as if you are wearing a blue pair of lenses, and thus the whole world looks blue. When you remove the blue lenses, the whole world looks and feels more colorful.

Beliefs begin as the result of our developing brain and nervous system being shaped by our earliest interactions with our caregivers. We are all born with the need to connect, to be seen, to be cared for, valued, and loved. If these needs are met, we develop healthy and positive beliefs about ourselves and the world. When our needs haven't been adequately met, we develop beliefs that may help us cope, but in the long run will limit or hurt us. Paula, in the above example, grew up believing that she was defective, that something was wrong with her. As a child, this belief was her way of understanding why she and her mother were abandoned by her father. But this deep-seated belief kept Paula from trying to improve her life.

Negative core beliefs lead to distorted thoughts—negative thoughts like Paula's interfere with our happiness and growth. In cognitive behavioral therapy (CBT), these types of thoughts are known as *cognitive distortions*. Here are some common examples:

**ALL-OR-NOTHING THINKING.** Also called black-and-white thinking, this is rigid thinking with no flexibility or middle ground.

**Examples:** *"You let me down. You must hate me. I'm no longer your friend." "All men are interested in only one thing." "If I don't attend everything I'm invited to, people will forget about me and I'll always be alone." "If I don't get all A's I'm stupid."*

**FILTERING.** This happens when we discount or filter out the positive and focus on the negative.

**Example:** *At a party where many people welcome you, you focus on the one or two people who didn't come up and say hello and conclude that no one wants you there.*

**OVERGENERALIZATION.** Making a sweeping conclusion based on a specific incident.

**Example:** *"Because I was turned down for that job, I know I'll always be rejected and never good enough for anyone to hire me."*

**"SHOULD" STATEMENTS.** Putting pressure on ourselves or others with statements that begin with "I should," "I must," "I need to," and similar language.

**Examples:** *"I should cook dinner every night; if not, I'm a bad mother." "My son should get all A's, otherwise he will be a failure in life."*

**MAGNIFYING/MINIMIZING.** Also known as catastrophizing/shrinking, this involves exaggerating mistakes (magnifying) or dismissing positive events or qualities (minimizing).

**Examples:** *"I forgot to call them back the same day. I'm a terrible person." "I only got a promotion because they couldn't find anyone else to do the work."*

**JUMPING TO CONCLUSIONS.** Judging something or making a decision based on minimal information, without having all the facts.

**Examples:** *"I saw my friend walking down the street and she didn't notice me; it must mean she's angry at me." "I know this guy I'm dating is going to dump me, and I'll never get married or have a family."*

**PERSONALIZATION OR BLAME.** You put all responsibility on yourself, or lay all the blame on another.

**Examples:** *"My mother was always ill; if I had just taken better care of her she would have lived longer." "If you made more money, our marriage wouldn't be in such trouble."*

**DISCOUNTING THE POSITIVES.** When you do something well, it doesn't count; you can't take in joy.

**Example:** *"The boss commended me for that report, but it was so simple anyone could have done it."*

**EMOTIONAL REASONING.** Acting and making decisions based on your emotions; believing that feelings are facts.

**Examples:** *"I feel insecure in my relationship, so I know my partner is cheating on me." "I feel afraid to drive; I know someone is going to hit me."*

**LABELING.** Judging others or ourselves based on a single characteristic, and seeing the whole person in that way.

**Examples:** *"I did poorly at that job interview; therefore, I'm a loser." "He rescheduled our date, so he is a flake."*

Do any of those thoughts sound familiar? When we identify and see the errors in our distorted thinking, we can replace these thoughts with new ones that are more affirming. This next exercise is designed to teach you how to identify your negative thoughts.

# HOW TO IDENTIFY THOUGHTS THAT HURT

The goal of this exercise is to help you become more familiar with your automatic negative thoughts. Recognizing an automatic thought can be an opportunity to explore it, ask for evidence, and then challenge the thought, helping you think differently.

Answer the questions below to identify some of the common negative thoughts you have about yourself. Since you're not used to noticing these thoughts, it may help to review the list above and imagine recent situations in which you felt bad about yourself. Try to come up with at least three examples for each question.

What do you say to yourself about your limitations or what you think you can achieve?

_____

_____

_____

What do you say to yourself about how others see you?

_____

_____

_____

What do you say to yourself about finding love?

_____

_____

_____

What do you say to yourself about your appearance?

_____

_____

_____

_____

If applicable, what do you say to yourself about your quality of parenting?

_____

_____

_____

_____

What do you say to yourself when you've made mistakes?

_____

_____

_____

_____

What do you say to yourself when you let someone down or someone lets you down?

_____

_____

_____

_____

What do you say to yourself about the bad things that have happened to you in your life that you don't want anyone else to know about?

_____

_____

_____

Feel free to add some other automatic thoughts here.

_____

_____

Now that you've identified some automatic negative thoughts, ask yourself: _Would I say these things to a friend or someone I love?_ Consider what you would say to that person instead.

When you notice automatic negative thoughts in your daily life, try to respond by speaking to yourself with the kindness and compassion you'd offer to a friend or loved one. Write down some of these compassionate responses below.

_____

_____

_____

Continue this practice by paying more attention to your thoughts during the course of your day. Most of us are very surprised to see how often we criticize or think negatively about ourselves or others. Along with paying more attention to automatic negative thoughts, try journaling about them to remind yourself of their frequency. You can use the chart on page 50 to track your automatic negative thoughts and pair each one with a compassionate response. This more compassionate or positive thought is often just the opposite of the negative thought. It's what you would say to a close friend if you heard them speaking negatively about themselves.

| DATE | SITUATION/ TRIGGER | AUTOMATIC NEGATIVE THOUGHT | COMPASSIONATE/ POSITIVE THOUGHT |
|------|--------------------|-----------------------------|----------------------------------|
|      |                    |                             |                                  |

## IMAGING POSSIBILITIES

The goal of this exercise is to begin to integrate new positive thoughts into our *felt sense* through putting them into practice. The felt sense is the internal experience of what we see, smell, taste, touch, hear—the integration of sensations, emotions, and meaning. Deepening our ability to integrate positive thoughts and create new neural pathways helps widen our window of tolerance.

1. Take one of your compassionate thoughts from your chart on the opposite page. Imagine how your life would be different if you fully, deeply, and unquestioningly believed this thought.

2. Close your eyes and picture a snapshot image that exemplifies this positive thought. Deepen the scenario by imagining who and what is in the picture. Notice the colors you see. Activate your other senses: Notice what you're hearing, what you might smell or touch with your fingers. What do you notice about yourself in this scene? What has changed for you? What is your felt sense?

3. Once you've established yourself in your mental snapshot, notice what's happening inside of you. What emotions and thoughts come with these new feelings?

After the exercise, write down any changes in your felt sense using the space below. As you begin to practice shifting negative thoughts to positive thoughts in your daily life, use this space or a journal to describe any progress. If you're having trouble, describe what's interfering.

Don't worry if you don't believe the positive thoughts that you recorded. They may feel foreign or untrue, but this is a process of changing deeply rooted thoughts that come from core beliefs. Those negative thoughts are like a deeply trodden path in the forest that you've always moved through easily. Now, we're working to forge a new path, which requires chopping through the old vines and clearing away brush. The new path is unfamiliar, but in time it will become trodden and comfortable as well. Swinging at those vines with a machete is hard work, but as the paths deepen and widen so too do the possibilities to see yourself and the world in a positive way.

# WHY OUR INTERNAL BELIEFS MATTER

Our core beliefs develop from our earliest interactions with our environment and provide a lens through which we view everything else. Sometimes our core beliefs are created even before we have language. Traumatic events may burden us with a sense of unease or shame, or an unnamed dread that we can't connect to any specific event or thought.

Our internal beliefs matter because we build relationships based on them. If our childhood has set us up to believe we are unlovable and unwanted, we may carry this belief throughout our lives and be unable to accept or see love. At the same time, we may be drawn into relationships with people who fit into our internal template. We don't realize it, but because certain people unconsciously feel like *home*, we keep experiencing the same neglect, abuse, or rejection patterns.

Rachel's parents were emotionally cold and physically absent from her childhood. She really raised herself. She was only praised for accomplishments at school and was expected to be perfect. Never having been loved for being her authentic self, but for only what she produced, Rachel grew up feeling she had to produce to be loved, and that she had to constantly protect herself from rejection. She kept her heart safe by finding fault with anyone who wanted to date her, rejecting them before they could reject her. The partners she felt most comfortable with were cold and distant. She kept herself extremely busy and felt the only love she could get was for what she accomplished in her career.

We try or don't try, take risks or don't take risks, based on internal core beliefs about ourselves, others, and the world. It's uncanny how trauma survivors unconsciously choose partners that in some way replicate what happened to them early on, reinforcing their core beliefs. In that way, their core beliefs become stronger.

Here are some examples of negative core beliefs, and how they can affect our thoughts.

| NEGATIVE CORE BELIEF | AUTOMATIC THOUGHTS |
| --- | --- |
| I don't deserve anything. | I expect to be passed over for promotions.<br><br>Families like mine can't expect anything good.<br><br>My family never had anything and I don't expect to either. |
| The world is not safe. | I always expect something bad to happen.<br><br>I must be prepared; I always know the other shoe is going to drop.<br><br>My parents taught me to always prepare for the worst.<br><br>I can't trust anyone; people will hurt me. |
| I'm unlovable. | I'll never find someone to marry me.<br><br>I don't even want to go to that party; I know people don't really want me there.<br><br>If I take care of others, they won't abandon me.<br><br>I expect to be lonely; I'm not worthy of love. |
| I'm bad. I'm defective. | I don't want to get close to others. If people really got to know me they would find out I'm bad.<br><br>I am to blame when things go wrong. I never do anything right. |
| I'm a burden. | I can't ask them to help me because I know they really wouldn't want to.<br><br>There is a cost to letting other people take care of you; you will owe them something.<br><br>No one has time for me. I'm just in the way. |
| I don't need; needs are bad. | Don't ask for help—you'll be perceived as weak.<br><br>I don't want to bother anyone. I learned as a little kid that people like you better if you don't ask for anything.<br><br>It's better to just accept what you have and not expect anything more.<br><br>I don't have time for frivolous feelings. |

*Table continues* ⟶

| NEGATIVE CORE BELIEF | AUTOMATIC THOUGHTS |
|---|---|
| My needs will never be met. | I'm always disappointed.<br><br>No one cares enough to be there for me—why should I even try? |
| People are not safe. | If I get too close to anyone I'll be hurt.<br><br>My father always taught me never to trust anyone.<br><br>Everyone I've ever gotten close to has always hurt me, starting with my parents. |
| I'm powerless. | I can't control anything in my life.<br><br>Nothing I do matters.<br><br>Every time I try to get ahead, I just get smashed back down. |

Our negative core beliefs have been with us for a very long time. They are so deeply rooted that they feel like truth. This makes it difficult to see other possibilities. These core beliefs were developed to protect us from being hurt, but now they are limiting us. We often find ourselves in a double bind: We have a great need for connection and closeness, yet at the same time have a belief that closeness is unsafe. This type of dilemma creates obstacles to change. But, now that you understand how these negative core beliefs developed, you can continue your journey toward freedom.

# IDENTIFYING YOUR CORE NEGATIVE BELIEFS

Now that you've seen how beliefs can negatively impact your sense of self and the world, this exercise will help you identify your negative core beliefs. Making these beliefs known is the next step to change. For example:

| NEGATIVE THOUGHT | NEGATIVE CORE BELIEF |
| --- | --- |
| *No one will ever love me.* | *I am unworthy of love.* |
| *My father taught me to never trust anyone.* | *The world is not safe.* |
| *Nothing I do matters. I will never amount to anything.* | *I'm powerless.* |

Referring to the thoughts you identified in the How to Identify Thoughts that Hurt exercise (page 47), list your automatic thoughts in the following chart. For each negative thought, add the core belief that the negative thought may have stemmed from.

| NEGATIVE THOUGHT | NEGATIVE CORE BELIEF |
| --- | --- |
|  |  |

After completing the chart, take a comfortable seat and focus on your breathing. Imagine a moment when you felt powerful or loved or accepted. If this is difficult, focus on the love you may have shared with a niece or nephew; feelings for a pet or favorite animal; your love for a piece of art or music; or the peace you've experienced while in nature. As you imagine this moment, take a snapshot and hold this in your mind's eye. Follow the steps of the Imagining Possibilities exercise (page 50) to put yourself into this snapshot of love and acceptance.

## UNDERSTANDING CORE BELIEFS AND TRIGGERS

This exercise is intended to help you more fully understand the impact of your core beliefs on your day-to-day life, which, in turn, will help you see how deeply negative core beliefs are affecting you so you can begin to believe differently.

Choose a typical day to try this exercise, and be aware of your negative thoughts and the core beliefs that correspond with those thoughts. Keep this book or a notebook with you. When you notice a situation that provokes or triggers a negative thought, record the details and try to connect it to a core belief. Here are some examples:

| TRIGGER/SITUATION | NEGATIVE AUTOMATIC THOUGHT | NEGATIVE CORE BELIEF |
|---|---|---|
| I lost my temper and yelled at my kids. | I'm a terrible parent. | I am bad. |
| I came to work today and my boss ignored me, and none of my coworkers spent time with me. | Nobody respects me; they don't like me very much. | I'm not good enough; I'm unlovable. |
| Every time I ask my husband for help, he yells at me to stop bothering him. | He never pays attention to me. | My needs will never be met. |
| I trusted my partner, and they cheated on me. | I can't trust anyone. | People are not safe. |
| People from my background never get ahead. | What's the use? | I'm powerless. |

Fill in the chart below by first identifying a trigger/situation, then the negative automatic thought that comes up, and finally the associated core belief. You can refer to the negative core beliefs you identified on page 55.

| TRIGGER/SITUATION | NEGATIVE AUTOMATIC THOUGHT | NEGATIVE CORE BELIEF |
|---|---|---|
|  |  |  |

Which core beliefs are most prominent in your life?

_____

_____


After the chart is compete, take a moment and repeat this affirmation to yourself:

*Awareness is the first step to change. Coming to understand my core beliefs will help me believe something more positive about myself and the world. I want to envision possibilities for myself that expand beyond my current limitations. I am on my way to developing new and healthier beliefs about myself and the world around me.*

## DEEPENING AWARENESS

Throughout this exercise, consider what you've learned about your core beliefs to deepen your understanding of how they hold you back and create distortions in your perceptions.

Answer the prompts below. Review previous exercises, if needed, to help you reflect on what you've learned.

When have your core beliefs held you back?

_____

_____


How have your core beliefs affected your relationships?

_____

_____

_____

How have you challenged your core beliefs?

_____

_____

_____

_____

How have your core beliefs negatively affected your sense of self?

_____

_____

_____

_____

What would you prefer to believe about yourself?

_____

_____

_____

_____

When you're finished, pause to reflect on this affirmation, repeating it out loud or
to yourself.

*The more I realize how my past has influenced my beliefs, the more I can trust
that my future can be free from these chains of the past. I do not have to continue
to believe these negative messages. I can choose to believe that I can heal.*

# April

April, a three-year-old child, seemed perfectly happy until her mother had a new baby. April's mother had a difficult pregnancy and had to remain in bed for the last three months before the birth of April's baby brother. April was told, "Shhhh, be quiet, you can't bother your mom, she's not well, leave her alone, go play, be a good girl." April couldn't understand what was wrong with her mother, and in her childlike way of seeing the world as all about herself, she began to believe that she was unwanted. She worried that she could hurt her mother if she bothered her, and that she was bad. Her negative core belief that she was bad created a sense of shame, along with anger that no one was there for her.

Young children are wired not to blame their parents, because they depend on them for survival, and blaming them would threaten that relationship. NARM therapy teaches that most survival strategies develop from the need to protect the attachment relationship. In that sense, the negative core belief of "I'm bad or unlovable" protected April—if it wasn't her parents' fault, the parent/child relationship could be preserved. April's belief that she's unlovable also protects her from rejection: She won't try to reach out, so no one can reject her. If she doesn't ask for anything, she can't be disappointed. As she grows older, these negative beliefs help April control her environment in order to shield her from being further wounded.

As April takes these core beliefs into adulthood, they become more limiting and problematic, causing issues with intimacy, inhibiting her connection with others, and contributing to her sense of unworthiness. As an adult in therapy, her work is to uncover her negative core beliefs, tracing the roots back to her childhood wounds and working through them in order to allow for something new.

# ROOTS OF NEGATIVE CORE BELIEFS

Now that you've come this far in your journey, in this exercise we'd like you to take another look at your genogram from chapter 2 (see page 31). You'll use the genogram to explore the intergenerational roots of your negative core beliefs. This will support your ability to uncouple what you inherited from the past so you can let it go in the present.

Using the list of your negative core beliefs from previous exercises (Identifying Your Core Negative Beliefs, page 55; Understanding Core Beliefs and Triggers, page 56), we'd like you to write about how these beliefs were passed down intergenerationally to you. If you didn't know your grandparents or great-grandparents, write about what you may have heard about them. Or, you can consider other important primary caregivers who may have influenced your development substantially.

Answer the questions below, using your genogram for reference.

How were your core beliefs communicated to you? Write down some examples from your memory. Go back as far as you can remember, describing events as a toddler, child, teenager, and young adult.

How did you see these beliefs play out in the lives of your parents?

How did you see these beliefs play out in the lives of your grandparents?

_____

_____

_____

_____

What do you know about how these beliefs might have played out in the lives of your great-grandparents?

_____

_____

_____

_____

Choose a core negative belief that you sense had the strongest impact on you, and describe how it's affected you.

_____

_____

_____

_____

Now that you've thought about the intergenerational roots of your core beliefs, you have the knowledge to separate out what is yours and what is theirs—that is, what belongs to the past and what belongs to you today. With that clarity comes hope to create new beliefs that are more accurate in the present. We'd like you to use the affirmation below daily to remind you that you can believe something new about yourself and the world. Repeat it to yourself three times, and allow the words to enter into your heart if you can. Consider adding the affirmation to your daily activity list.

*My history does not define me. I can create new beliefs.*
*I can create a new story.*

# CHALLENGING NEGATIVE CORE BELIEFS

You've examined how negative core beliefs impact your life, so now let's look at how your life would be different with new beliefs. Challenging your beliefs will help you develop healthier neural pathways. For this exercise, work with the negative core beliefs you identified previously.

1.  Identify three of your most prominent negative core beliefs and the corresponding positive beliefs.

2.  For each positive belief, create three short-term goals. These should be actions you can take that demonstrate the positive belief.

Examples of positive core beliefs:

I deserve good things.

The world is mostly safe.

I'm lovable.

I'm a good person.

I can make mistakes and accept that it's okay to ask for help.

Needs are part of my humanness.

There are ways to get needs met.

Mostly people are safe.

I can make things happen.

Here's a format you can use to record your goals:

**NEGATIVE BELIEF:** *I'm unlovable.*

**POSITIVE BELIEF:** *I'm lovable.*

**GOALS:** 1.      *I'm lovable, therefore it is safe to smile and look people in the eye when I see them.*

     2.      *I'm lovable, therefore I will initiate conversation with people I want to be friends with.*

     3.      *I'm lovable, therefore I can speak up when my partner does something I don't like, without worrying that they'll reject me.*

**NEGATIVE BELIEF:** *People are not safe.*

**POSITIVE BELIEF:** *People are mostly safe.*

**GOALS:** 1.      *People are mostly safe, so if my boss is in a bad mood, I will not assume it's about me.*

     2.      *People are mostly safe, therefore I will not panic when I leave my house.*

     3.      *People are mostly safe, and I will choose to associate with people who respect me and my boundaries.*

Use the lines below to record your negative beliefs, positive beliefs, and goals.

**NEGATIVE BELIEF #1:** _____

**POSITIVE BELIEF** _____

**GOALS:** 1.      _____

     2.      _____

     3.      _____

## NEGATIVE BELIEF #2: _____

**POSITIVE BELIEF** _____

**GOALS: 1.** _____

    **2.** _____

    **3.** _____

## NEGATIVE BELIEF #3: _____

**POSITIVE BELIEF** _____

**GOALS: 1.** _____

    **2.** _____

    **3.** _____

It takes time to shift deeply rooted beliefs. Although practicing these new behaviors may feel artificial or awkward at first, over time the results will be surprisingly positive and freeing. If a goal turns out to be too ambitious, don't blame yourself. Scale it back, take baby steps, and keep practicing.

Practice these goals for 30 days, keeping track on your calendar, and take note how things have changed at the end of the 30 days. Maybe the change is small, but remember that every long journey is made up of small steps.

# INTEGRATING YOUR NEW BELIEFS

In the space below, describe what it's been like integrating positive beliefs into your daily life. As you listen to your thoughts, hear a negative belief being expressed and then intentionally shift to the opposite, positive belief, what do you notice? How has this affected your sense of self or others? How have your new beliefs impacted your relationship with your family, your friends, or your workplace colleagues? What have you learned about your negative core beliefs? What have you learned while trying on alternative positive beliefs?

Keep practicing daily, noticing negative thoughts and negative beliefs and then replacing them with positive beliefs and positive actions where you can. Keeping a daily journal can really help you on this journey.

# LOVING KINDNESS MEDITATION

As you work on identifying negative beliefs, negative thoughts, and their roots, you may start noticing that you feel anger toward your family or about your past. This can feel overwhelming or surprising; you might find yourself holding conflicting feelings of love and anger. Or maybe there is only anger. Sometimes family members did the best they could but still caused us harm. Sometimes they may have been outright abusive. Either way, this can be tricky to navigate, and if the feelings become too strong you may need the help of a professional.

One way to soothe these feelings and stay connected to feelings of self-compassion and self-love is with the following loving kindness meditation.

1. Begin by grounding yourself. Sit comfortably and notice the feeling of your feet on the ground, the sensation of your body in the chair. Notice your breathing; feel your belly rise and fall.

2. Straighten your back, allowing your spine to stretch as if it is being gently held from above.

3. Repeat the following series of phrases three times, allowing yourself to take in each word. See if you can notice how the words make you feel inside. You can place one hand on your heart and one hand on your belly as you say the words silently or aloud.

*May I be happy. May I be safe. May I be loved.*

As you hear your words, try to sense what it feels like to feel happy, safe, and loved. Where do you notice the feeling in your body, in your heart, in your head, and in your belly?

4. If you like, repeat the phrases while directing loving kindness toward specific people, to family, to friends, to animals and nature:

*May you be happy. May you be safe. May you be loved.*

**5.** Complete this loving kindness practice by returning to yourself with compassion, repeating the phrases:

*May I be happy. May I be safe. May I be loved.*

As you finish your meditation, see if you can practice what is called a dual-awareness: Hold on to the calm presence of the loving kindness meditation for as long as you can while returning to the activities of your day.

It would be wonderful to practice this meditation on a regular basis!

# CHAPTER HIGHLIGHTS

- Our thoughts, feelings, and behaviors influence and interact with each other.

- Distorted thoughts have roots in early distress and serve as an attempt to make sense of early negative experiences.

- Negative thoughts are often so automatic we barely notice them and accept them as fact.

- Negative automatic thoughts can be challenged by developing alternative positive thoughts.

- Core beliefs develop from our earliest interactions and provide a lens through which we view everything else.

- Our core beliefs profoundly affect how we experience self, others, and the world.

- By identifying negative core beliefs and negative automatic thoughts, we empower ourselves to change to positive thoughts and beliefs.

- Challenging core beliefs is crucial for change and may also bring up new and uncomfortable feelings.

# CHAPTER 4

# MANAGING YOUR EMOTIONS

Emotions let us know how we are interpreting information that comes from our senses. They're signals that alert us to what's happening and what we should pay attention to: fear can warn us of danger, anger can prepare us for conflict, sadness can allow us to grieve, and loneliness can tell us it's time to reach out for connection. Joy and happiness and love are signals that we are alive, vibrant, and connected. Healthy emotional development enables these signals to function properly and equips us to understand and deal with them effectively. But trauma interferes with this development.

Trauma survivors often have a heightened struggle with managing their emotions, so in this chapter we'll focus on exercises and reflections to support your ability to do just that. We'll explore how trauma keeps us from really knowing our feelings, how to effectively label our emotions, and ways to handle emotional triggers. You'll learn strategies for emotional regulation, and you'll complete exercises that will help you develop comfort with your feelings by staying in your window of tolerance.

# UNDERSTANDING YOUR EMOTIONS

Infants are born with primary emotions and the ability to sense their physical needs. Most researchers believe that babies are born with nine basic emotions from birth, as evidenced in babies' facial expressions: interest (or curiosity), enjoyment, surprise, distress, anger, fear, shame, disgust (literally a reaction to noxious tastes), and "dissmell" (a similar reaction to noxious odors). As infants develop into toddlers, then into children, their range of emotions expands.

We're not born with a thinking brain, so early in our lives it's emotional cues that provide information to our primary caretakers about our needs. Human infants are born without the capacity to regulate or manage their emotions: When a baby feels frightened, angry, or surprised, they experience the emotion with no way to do anything about it. Infants have no ability to think about, understand, or change their feelings or sensations. Parents don't always know this, but one of their primary roles is to help regulate, or manage, the emotions in their infant. For example, a hungry newborn cries, signaling that they need to be fed. The infant is powerless to make the bad feelings go away. If fed, the baby's emotional reaction becomes positive. If not fed, they're left helpless in this unregulated state. And if they are consistently left in that unregulated state—possibly because a parent's experience of trauma inhibits their caregiving—the infant may shut down, disconnecting from all emotions as a habitual defense against negative feelings. Of course, no parent will ever be perfect and meet their infant's needs 100 percent of the time. Researchers have found that doing so most of the time—being a "good enough parent"—does the trick.

As an infant grows and language develops, the parent's role broadens to helping the child understand what they are feeling. One of the ways they do this is by naming their emotions. For example, suppose a child is crying over losing a favorite toy. Ideally, a parent might say something like, "You're feeling sad, aren't you? You don't like it when you lose something that you really love." When parents put a name to their child's feeling, it becomes less scary. The child begins to understand the emotion they are experiencing, and they feel less out of control. But a parent who's impaired by trauma might say, "Stop your crying, you have nothing to cry about," or nothing at all.

In a trauma-burdened family, where feelings haven't been encouraged or allowed, children either don't learn to understand their feelings or feel shame for even having these feelings. They learn to avoid feelings in general by shutting them down or pushing them away. But buried emotions don't go away. Suppressed emotions can come out in different ways. They can produce physical or mental illness; they can become under-expressed (hypoarousal, or numbness and dissociation) or over-expressed (hyperarousal; that is, agitation, panic, anger, rage, or anxiety).

Our early interactions of our needs being met, or of experiencing neglect or abuse, create a template of expectation. We expect to feel what we already felt, and similar situations can become a trigger for this expectation and the corresponding emotion. People who've experienced trauma generally develop an oversensitive nervous system and respond to triggers in a heightened way—because they're actually responding from their template, from their history. Trauma survivors are often hypervigilant, always on guard, expecting threats. They might react to a teakettle whistle as if they were hearing a fire alarm.

Melody was physically and sexually abused by her uncle, a large man who was a construction worker. As an adult, anytime she sees a construction worker she feels fear, as if she is in danger. Melody knows, logically, that not all construction workers are dangerous. But seeing one triggers an emotional reaction rooted in her early trauma. With the help of trauma-informed therapy, Melody became able to pause this reaction. This allows her to more accurately assess the current situation and whether there's an actual threat.

# GETTING BETTER ACQUAINTED WITH YOUR FEELINGS

For this exercise, we want to teach you how to know your feelings. Recall that by putting a name to feelings we can feel more in control. There are two steps that support this process:

1.  Noticing the signals from your body that help you clarify what you are feeling.

2.  Putting a name to the feelings, which is the first step in being able to regulate or resolve them and thus feel more in control.

Connecting your body and your feelings is an important step toward healthy functioning. In this exercise, you'll practice using physical sensations to help you name and identify your emotions.

Following is a list of some basic emotions and ways that they're signaled by sensations of the body. You may experience other sensations; feel free to add to the list.

Review the list and circle the sensations and emotions that apply to you most often.

Remember, not everyone feels all the sensations associated with a particular emotion, and everyone's experience of sensation and emotions may be different.

Once you've worked through the list, answer the questions below by noting what signals and sensations tell you that you are having that feeling. You can apply the questions to other emotions as well.

What tells you that you're angry?

_____

_____

What tells you that you're feeling love?

_____

_____

| PHYSICAL SENSATIONS<br>*Sensations I might be feeling . . .* | EMOTION<br>*They may mean*<br>*I'm experiencing . . .* |
| --- | --- |
| Expanded, Electric, Flowing, Fluttery, Radiating, Releasing, Spacious, Tingling, Vibrating, Warm | Joy |
| Expanded, Flowing, Fluid, Loose, Radiating, Relaxed, Settled, Spacious, Vibrating, Warm | Happiness |
| Calm, Excited, Expanded, Gentle, Invigorated, Light, Open, Radiating, Sensitive, Soft, Spacious, Tender, Warm | Love |
| Airy, Expanded, Flowing, Fluid, Gentle, Light, Relaxed, Settled, Slow, Soft, Spacious, Still, Warm | Calm |
| Breathless, Dizzy, Electric, Expanded, Flowing, Fluttery, Pulsing, Radiating, Spacious, Warm | Excitement |
| Breathless, Clenched, Constricted, Frozen, Knotted, Nauseous, Jumpy, Pounding, Sweaty, Tense, Tight, Twitchy, Wobbly | Fear |
| Blocked, Cold, Drained, Empty, Frozen, Heavy, Hollow, Knotted, Nauseous, Numb, Pained, Sensitive, Sore | Sadness |
| Clenched, Constricted, Queasy, Pulsing, Sensitive, Shaky | Disgust |
| Burning, Clenched, Hot, Pounding, Prickly, Rigid, Shaky, Throbbing, Tight, Trembling, Twitchy, Vibrating | Anger |
| Breathless, Buzzed, Electric, Expanded, Fluttery, Jumpy, Pulsing, Radiating, Shaky, Shivering, Tingly | Surprise |
| Breathless, Burning, Buzzed, Clammy, Clenched, Constricted, Dizzy, Electric, Fluttery, Hot, Itchy, Jumpy, Knotted, Nauseous, Pained, Pounding, Prickly, Pulsing, Radiating, Sensitive, Shaky, Shivery, Suffocated, Sweaty, Tense, Throbbing, Tight, Trembly, Twitching, Wobbly | Anxious |
| Blocked, Bruised, Constricted, Dull, Empty, Heavy, Hollow, Knotted, Numb, Pained, Rigid, Sensitive, Sore, Stiff, Wooden | Lonely |
| Blocked, Bruised, Burning, Clenched, Constricted, Contained, Frozen, Hot, Pained, Pulsing, Sensitive, Shaky, Sweaty, Vibrating | Shame |

What tells you that you're happy?

_____

_____

What tells you that you're sad?

_____

_____

What tells you that you're feeling afraid?

_____

_____

What tells you that you're anxious?

_____

_____

What tells you that you're feeling miserable?

_____

_____

What tells you that you're feeling calm?

_____

_____

Extend this exercise throughout your day by checking in with yourself. Periodically, take your emotional temperature: Imagine a temperature gauge, with 0 being calm and 10 being the red zone: full-blown rage, panic, fear, hopelessness, or other negative emotions. Where are you on this gauge? If you're in the red, take some time to practice calming yourself with one of the meditations in this book, or by taking some deep breaths and noticing something pleasant in your environment. Look at some beautiful artwork, listen to calming music, or go somewhere that has a soothing effect, if only in your mind's eye.

## YOUR EMOTIONAL TRIGGERS

Knowing what situations trigger your emotions will help you recognize when you're operating outside of your window of tolerance. Whenever you have an emotional reaction that seems more than what's called for in the moment (a fire alarm reaction to a teakettle situation), you're generally reacting to history. Identification of these triggers is the first step in being able to rightsize your emotional responses. Recognizing that particular situations cause big emotions, you can begin to identify your triggers and examine how your overreactions cause problems.

Here are some examples of triggers:

Your boss speaks to you in a loud tone.

Your child doesn't listen to you.

A person of a similar type to your abuser is in your vicinity.

Someone with authority asks you to do something or criticizes you.

**Example:** *I feel anxious when my boss asks to speak with me, and this causes me to get a panicked feeling inside, making me nauseated and scared.*

**Example:** *I feel angry when someone judges my actions, and this causes me to escalate from 0 to 10, screaming at everyone around me.*

Think about situations that cause you emotional distress, and fill in the blanks below to describe your triggers and emotional or behavioral reaction.

**TRIGGER #1:**   I feel anxious when _____,

_____

and this causes me to _____

_____.

**TRIGGER #2:**   I feel angry when _____,

_____

and this causes me to _____

_____.

**TRIGGER #3:**   I feel rejected when _____,

_____

and this causes me to _____

_____.

**TRIGGER #4:**   I feel fear when _____,

_____

and this causes me to _____

_____.

**TRIGGER #5:**   I feel shame when _____,

_____

and this causes me to _____

_____.

**TRIGGER #6:**   I feel depressed when _____,

_____

and this causes me to _____

_____.

TRIGGER #7:   I feel hopeless when _____,

_____

and this causes me to _____

_____.

It's equally valuable to reflect on situations that bring positive emotions. Negative emotions stay with us, whereas positive ones can be more difficult to hold on to. How often have you replayed a negative situation over and over in your head? Let's do the same for our positives. Reflect on a moment of joy, and notice the emotions and sensations you feel. Recall what caused the joy. Knowing that you had this experience, tell yourself that you are capable of having it again.

Make a practice of reflecting on a positive emotion anytime you find yourself rerunning a negative experience in your mind.

## FAMILY EMOTIONS

This exercise will help you further identify the way emotions were expressed, honored, ignored, or criticized in your family. Becoming more familiar with the roots of our emotions helps us uncouple the past from the present and respond in emotionally healthy ways. Additionally, if we understand how a parent's negative reaction to our feelings affected our ability to feel, we can then work through what is holding us back from experiencing a full range of emotions.

Answer the questions below, applying them to your childhood.

As a child, how did your family and others help you name and be present with your feelings?

_____

_____

_____

_____

How did your family respond to your feelings? What were some typical statements, positive or negative? (For example, "You're being a crybaby." versus "Come over here and tell me what has you so upset.")

_____

_____

_____

_____

What did you learn about your feelings from these responses?

_____

_____

_____

_____

How was anger expressed in your family?

_____

_____

_____

How was love expressed? If it wasn't, write about that.

_____

_____

_____

_____

If you were hurt or afraid, what did you do? Who would you talk to?

_____

_____

_____

_____

What was the emotional connection between your grandparents and parents?

_____

_____

_____

_____

What was your emotional connection to your grandparents?

_____

_____

_____

_____

What was your emotional connection to your parents?

_____

_____

_____

_____

What topics were off-limits for discussion?

_____

_____

_____

_____

How were needs expressed—or not—in your family?

_____

_____

_____

_____

Did you feel valued in your family? If yes, what made you feel that way? If not, write about that.

_____

_____

_____

_____

Did you feel safe in your family? Write about what made you feel safe or unsafe. (If you were abused or neglected, these questions can be quite triggering; you don't need to go into the details.)

_____

_____

_____

_____

After completing the questions, take a moment to reflect. Now that you've identified the roots of some of your emotions, it can be helpful to remind yourself through daily affirmations that you can change your emotional legacy. Say the following affirmation out loud or to yourself daily. Perhaps make it part of your morning routine.

*I am committed to uncoupling the past from the present, to learning new and healthier ways to deal with my emotions, and I know that healing is possible. As I take a deeper look at where my emotional patterns have come from, I acknowledge that I am from my family, but I am not my family.*

# Melody

Melody, who we mentioned earlier, came to therapy to deal with childhood sexual and physical abuse. Nighttime and darkness caused her to become extremely anxious; often she couldn't sleep, and she'd have terrible nightmares. Melody was single and hadn't had any long-term relationships. She talked about her fear of men who were physically large; the few boyfriends she did have were people she felt she could control. She had been in love only once, but the relationship ended because he was abusive. Melody reported that when in the presence of a large man, even if just walking down the street, her heart would beat rapidly, and she'd feel an overwhelming urge to run. She had even dropped or switched classes in college because the professor was a large male; she couldn't tolerate the feelings of anxiety and panic she felt in their proximity.

Melody described her childhood self as being seen but not heard. She and her sister were hit by their father if they misbehaved. Melody was never sure if her mother knew that her uncle sexually abused her; Melody never told anyone. No one ever asked about feelings or talked about feelings in Melody's home. Both her parents had lived difficult, impoverished lives that had impaired their capacity for nurturing.

During therapy, Melody came to realize that even though she often felt unsafe, in reality she was reacting to her past abuse. Identifying triggers such as going to bed, physically large men, and nighttime helped her connect her present-day symptoms to the past trauma. She learned that, though she had no one to protect her as a child, as an adult she now had the ability to keep herself safe. Aware of her triggers, she could change the emotional responses that were no longer appropriate for the present. Regulating her emotions enabled Melody to develop new neural pathways, empowering her with new ways of reacting to her triggers.

# UNDERSTANDING EMOTIONAL REGULATION

When your emotions are all over the place—that is, *dysregulated*—your life can feel hijacked by their intensity. When you are constantly feeling triggered, your day-to-day life and relationships are affected, and you often feel out of control. It's like being in the ocean in a storm, in a small lifeboat with no oars and no life preserver, fearing for your life.

Emotional regulation is your ability to shift or manage the intensity of your emotions, to return to the window of tolerance when you're feeling stressed. When you can regulate your emotions, you're able to take the oars of your boat and move in the direction you choose. As we discussed previously, early interactions between parent and infant are crucial for the infant's ability to regulate their emotions throughout life. Individuals who have experienced intergenerational trauma struggle with their emotions because their regulation system hasn't been set up. The regulation system includes both co-regulation (relational) and self-regulation (self-soothing). Parents who because of trauma did not develop emotional regulation strategies generally cannot adequately regulate their developing child's emotions.

When we don't learn to manage our emotions, we can develop maladaptive strategies—ineffective or problematic ways of coping with emotion—instead. For example, someone who comes to therapy for anger management may find they never learned to regulate anger because of their parents' explosive behavior. Dysregulated emotion can also show up in the form of panic attacks, autoimmune disorders, high blood pressure, gastrointestinal problems, chronic pain, rage storms, explosive behavior, difficulty with activities of daily living, paranoia, hypervigilance, or feelings of defeat, numbness, emptiness, or isolation. Other symptoms are more relational, with relationship problems due to misperceiving others, reacting to the present as if it were the past, being easily offended or intolerant to criticism, or a lack of the ability to trust.

Asha had highly critical parents with high expectations. She came to therapy because of pressure from her girlfriend. She reported that she has difficulty in most personal relationships because she is easily offended, misperceives criticism from everyone, and becomes highly dysregulated when she feels criticized, her emotional temperature going from 0 to 10. This has made her current relationship problematic, because Asha always feels that her girlfriend is criticizing her. Asha had to learn how her distorted perceptions, coupling the past with the present, were causing her emotions to spike.

Learning healthier ways to manage your emotions requires taking a good look at the strategies you are currently using. Once you identify unhealthy strategies, the next step is to identify healthy alternatives and begin practicing them.

# STRATEGIES TO REGULATE EMOTIONS

Trauma survivors may develop maladaptive ways of managing their emotions, such as abusing alcohol or drugs; overeating; overspending; sexual compulsivity; codependency; workaholism; gambling; raging; oversleeping; compulsive use of video gaming, online pornography, or other technology; self-harm; and isolation.

In this exercise, we'd like you to examine the current strategies you use to regulate your strong emotions, and what you would like to change. This identification is the first step toward learning to regulate your emotions to return you to the window of tolerance. When we're outside that window—in hyper- or hypoarousal—we don't always see things as they are, but instead as we project them to be. Part of emotional regulation is seeing things as they are, in the moment, uncoupled from the trauma of the past.

Here are some healthy ways to manage your emotions:

- Come back to the present moment
- Pause
- Take a bubble bath
- Go for a walk
- Slow yourself down
- Talk to a calming family member or friend
- Play with your pet
- Notice and name objects in your surroundings
- Use a heating pad on your shoulders or under the arches of your feet
- Light a scented candle
- Use an aromatherapy diffuser
- Play soothing music

- Count backward from 100 by seven
- Hold an ice cube
- Take belly breaths
- Feel the sensation of your feet against the ground
- Use a weighted blanket
- Make some art
- Read
- Go outside in nature
- Follow a guided visualization or meditation
- Exercise
- Give yourself a butterfly hug (cross your hands over your chest, and alternately tap each hand against your shoulders).

Add your own ideas for healthy strategies below:

- _____
- _____
- _____

Complete the write-in exercise below, describing five emotions, your physical reactions, and a healthier way to respond (from the list above or your own suggestion). Use this template for your answer:

When I feel _____, I _____, and then I
            _EMOTION_           _PHYSICAL RESPONSE_

_____
_CURRENT STRATEGY TO REGULATE MY EMOTIONS_

A healthy strategy I could use instead is: _____
                                      _HEALTHY ADAPTIVE STRATEGY TO REGULATE EMOTION_

_____

**Example:**

_When I feel angry, I start to notice my breath changes, I want to throw something, and I feel out of control, and then I tend to overeat to calm myself down._

_A healthy strategy I could use instead is: I would like to be able to slow myself down (pause), then take a bubble bath._

**Example:**

_When I feel scared, I start to notice my heart pounding and my thoughts racing, and then I grab a drink and keep drinking._

_A healthy strategy I could use instead is: calm myself by coming back to the present moment and noticing where I am and what is around me, and that there is no immediate danger._

## EMOTION #1:

When I feel _____,
          *EMOTION*

I _____,
   *PHYSICAL RESPONSE*

and then I _____.
           *CURRENT STRATEGY TO REGULATE MY EMOTIONS*


A healthy strategy I could use instead is:


_____

*HEALTHY ADAPTIVE STRATEGY TO REGULATE EMOTION*

_____


## EMOTION #2:

When I feel _____,

I _____,

and then I _____.


A healthy strategy I could use instead is:


_____

_____


## EMOTION #3:

When I feel _____,

I _____,

and then I _____.

A healthy strategy I could use instead is:

_____

_____

## EMOTION #4:

When I feel _____ ,

I _____ ,

and then I _____ .

A healthy strategy I could use instead is:

_____

_____

## EMOTION #5:

When I feel _____ ,

I _____ ,

and then I _____ .

A healthy strategy I could use instead is:

_____

_____

As a next step, try to notice when your feelings become dysregulated by noticing both your feelings and your physical response. Then, try one of your new strategies. To start, you may want to create a list of healthy strategies that you can review when you need it. Practice using one strategy daily. Try not to judge yourself when you find yourself reverting to an old habit. Be compassionate with yourself and keep trying. These new strategies will become easier with practice.

## FEELING JUST A BIT AT A TIME

In this exercise, we want to help you learn to feel your feelings, but without overwhelming yourself. You'll use a strategy called *distancing* to control the intensity of your feelings. Distancing involves using a mental image to slow down your response, push the emotion further away, watch the emotion pass by, or take a pause to change the intensity of your feelings.

There are several mental images you can use:

- Imagine yourself sitting in a train, watching through the window and seeing the scenery go by, with your distressing mental image as a part of the scenery that's receding away—so that there is space between you and the distressing image.

- Imagine yourself sitting along the bank of a river, watching the distressing image float on the river's current, drifting farther away from you.

- Project an imagined picture of your thoughts and emotions onto a wall. Then use a remote control to make the picture smaller, quiet the volume, pause the images, or shut it off completely.

- Imagine a large wall or shield between you and the disturbing emotions and images.

  1. Decide which of the above distancing techniques you would like to use for this first practice.

  2. Settle yourself into a comfortable sitting position. Focus attention on the sensations of breathing, of your feet on the ground, and your body on the chair. You can close your eyes or keep them open and focused on one spot.

3.  Visualize yourself having to wait at the end of a very long line, on a very hot day, with pushy people behind you bumping up against you. Notice the frustration, the sensations, and the emotions that begin to bubble up. If this doesn't elicit frustration, bring to your mind's eye a memory of a recent time when you felt frustration or anxiety. Choose something only moderately distressing, since this is your first practice with distancing techniques.

4.  Holding your distressing situation in your mind's eye, see if you can slow down the feelings with one of the distancing techniques described at the beginning of this exercise. See the upsetting emotions passing by or being paused, reduced, or blocked.

5.  Make sure you stay grounded in the moment, returning attention to your breathing as needed, while keeping the distress at a distance.

6.  Gently open or relax your eyes and bring yourself back into the present.

Take a moment to reflect. What was this distancing practice like for you? Did you notice a shift in your feelings? Were you able to control the intensity? Which distancing technique did you choose? You may want to try them all. After you've had some practice, see if you can use distancing whenever uncomfortable emotions start to become too intense in your daily life. By learning to distance our emotions, we can increase our capacity to regulate our feelings.

## NURTURING IMAGE MINDFULNESS PRACTICE

For those who have experienced trauma, quieting the mind may be quite difficult. You may not have experienced enough nurturing, making it difficult to feel loved or cared for. As taught in attachment-focused EMDR, using an imagined nurturer as a resource can evoke positive feelings that otherwise aren't available to you. The concept is similar to a basketball player imagining standing at the free throw line, shooting, and seeing the ball go in the basket to improve their free throw. It's another way of building and strengthening new, healthy neural pathways in your brain.

1. Find a comfortable sitting position.

2. You can close your eyes or focus on one spot in the room.

3. Ground yourself by noticing your feet on the ground and feeling your body on the seat.

4. Begin to notice your breathing.

5. Try to relax any places in your body where you're feeling stress or tension.

6. Bring to your mind's eye a figure who elicits a feeling of support and nurturing. This can be someone real or imagined; human, animal, or fantastical; it could be someone from the past or present, a fictional character, someone you know or have never met. Do not choose a primary caretaker, or someone who doesn't always make you feel good, since that could bring up negative associations or an unpleasant emotional reaction.

7. Imagine this figure having nurturing qualities. Imagine the figure with all your senses, what they'd look like, sound like, smell like, and how their nurturing characteristics would be expressed. They might have a loving, melodic voice; a calm and approachable demeanor; compassionate eyes; and an empathetic touch. For example, Mrs. Weasley from Harry Potter, Nana from Peter Pan, Mother Nature, or the loving part of you.

8. Sit with the resource you've imagined and its nurturing qualities, and take in its presence. What do you notice about being in its company? Notice any shift in your emotions. What has changed?

As a next step, imagine this resource is available to you whenever you are in need of love or nurturing. Remember that every time you evoke this nurturing presence in your imagination, it can help create new pathways in your brain, strengthening your ability to feel calm and nurtured. Practice imagining this resource when you're not triggered emotionally so you can access it more easily when you most need it. You don't need to sit with your resource for a long period of time; five to ten minutes is usually sufficient, though you can spend more time if you want.

# UNDERSTANDING AVOIDANCE

Dysregulated feelings can manifest in ways that make a person feel out of control with panic, fear, and/or anxiety. But trauma can evoke another response to emotions: avoidance. Someone who's been affected by trauma may avoid emotions and situations that might trigger them so they're protected from overwhelming feelings of terror, rage, loss of control, and powerlessness. Avoidance is also a means to prevent reliving a traumatic event over and over again.

Avoidance can be a conscious or unconscious way of managing feelings. Someone might avoid conversations, staying away from discussions or people that elicit undesirable feelings. Avoiding relationships, or sabotaging them, can be a way to keep emotions at a distance. A person may become numb, spaced-out, or dissociated when exposed to reminders of their trauma. In extreme cases, avoidance can lead to a disconnection from any internal awareness of self or history (dissociation), sometimes even a blacking out of the memory of past trauma.

We all use avoidance at times and to various degrees. If something is really troubling, a common avoidance strategy may be to say, "I don't want to think about this," and put it off until later. Sometimes we need to be able to push something away and go on about our day.

Avoidance becomes maladaptive or troubling when the strategy we are using to avoid the emotion causes problems for us. Strategies like overeating, excess drinking, over-work, drug abuse, and self-isolation can interfere with our daily life and can be signs of post-traumatic stress disorder. In extreme cases, avoidance can cause a feeling of being foggy, spacey, tuned out, numb, or disconnected when traumatic memories are triggered. In addition, someone might feel as if they're outside of their body, detached as an observer (depersonalization), or experience the world as unreal (derealization).

Heather, a 45-year-old female, came into therapy to deal with her pattern of codependent abusive relationships. Heather was in recovery but felt her life worked better when she was drinking; it was much easier for her to end relationships and to never become deeply emotionally attached. She described several recent boyfriends who physically abused her. Later in therapy, she was able to share that her father had sexually abused her. When she discussed the details, she had no emotion. Heather had big gaps in her memory, and sometimes during therapy she would become foggy, confused, and break eye contact. She would stop and ask, "What did you say? I got lost for a minute." It became clear that Heather was dissociating in therapy sessions, had dissociated during most of the sexual abuse by her father, and continues dissociating with her present abusive relationships.

## MY AVOIDANCE SYMPTOMS

Avoiding emotions doesn't make them go away. Recognizing difficult feelings and being able to deal with them in a healthy way is an important step in healing from trauma. In this exercise, let's examine feelings and situations that you may be currently avoiding so you can learn to better manage them.

Write about one emotion that you may avoid that has some connection to trauma. If an emotion tends to occur in overwhelming intensity, too big for the situation, you can suspect that trauma is involved.

How does avoiding this emotion cause positive or negative results?

Is there a situation you avoid that has some connection to trauma?

How does avoiding this cause positive or negative results?

_____

_____

_____

Are there people you avoid who have some connection to trauma?

_____

_____

_____

How does avoiding them cause positive or negative results?

_____

_____

_____

Is there a place that you avoid that has some connection to trauma?

_____

_____

_____

How does avoiding it cause positive or negative results?

_____

_____

_____

Is there a memory you avoid talking about that has some connection to trauma?

_____

_____

_____

How does avoiding it cause positive or negative results?

_____

_____

_____

When you're finished, reflect for a bit on your responses, then answer the prompts below:

What does this tell you about how avoidance affects you and your relationships and quality of life? Can you imagine responding differently without avoidance?

Can you imagine ways in which your life might be different without the avoidance? Describe below.

_____

_____

_____

_____

_____

_____

_____

## IT HAPPENED TO . . .

Avoiding distressing emotions has the harmful consequence of dampening positive feelings as well. When we restrict or avoid feelings, that can include all feelings, good and bad, happy and sad. Conversely, learning to allow ourselves to feel, not avoid, opens up our capacity for aliveness and connectedness. But this may not be an easy task if you've practiced long and hard to avoid painful feelings. Sometimes it's easier to feel emotions relating to another person than to ourselves, which is the concept behind this next exercise.

In the space below, write the story of your childhood as if you were writing about someone else. Keeping the history and details the same, tell the story as if it happened to a different child. (For example, "She grew up in a large family," instead of "I grew up in a large family.") How do you imagine the child is feeling? What do you feel for this child? What might you like to say to this child? Do you feel compassion for the child? Do you feel contempt? Do you feel love? Let whatever comes up, come up. Use the self-regulation exercises you've been practicing to help you return to the window of tolerance if you start to feel overwhelmed. Continue on another piece of paper if you run out of space.

When you've finished the story, reflect on any differences between the way you feel for the child in the story and the way you feel about yourself. As you do this, what do you notice? If this exercise is too difficult or too painful, put it aside for now and consider that you might need therapy or other support to allow yourself to access these avoided feelings.

# CHAPTER HIGHLIGHTS

- Emotions are how our senses help us interpret information.

- One primary role of parents is to help regulate emotions in their infant; when this goes well, the child learns to manage their emotions as they get older.

- Parents with unresolved trauma, without the capacity to regulate their own emotions, may pass down emotional dysregulation to their children.

- Putting a name to their emotions helps children learn healthy emotional expression.

- Infants develop a template of expectation and emotional responses from which they will perceive everything after that. Later in life, situations that echo past traumatic experiences can trigger oversized emotions because we are really reacting to the past.

- Emotional regulation keeps us in the window of tolerance—not too high and not too low—and able to see things "clearly" from the present.

- Dysregulated emotions can be expressed as hyperarousal (panic, anger, rage, fear) or hypoarousal (numbness, depression, dissociation).

- Avoidance can be conscious and unconscious. Avoidance is a protective strategy for dealing with painful emotions, memories, or reminders of trauma. We protect ourselves by avoiding certain conversations, situations, people, feelings, and memories.

- Distancing helps us experience our emotions without allowing them to overwhelm us.

# CHAPTER 5

# HEALING YOUR BODY

No discussion of trauma would be complete without talking about ways to heal trauma's effects on the body. Traditionally, body and mind have been treated separately, ignoring the understanding that mind and body are intrinsically connected. As we review the connection between mind and body in this chapter, you'll see how self-care supports healing the brain and nervous system from the effects of trauma. Incorporating self-care in your daily life not only improves your physical well-being, it also promotes the development of new neural pathways that are so important for trauma survivors' healing.

# TRAUMA'S PHYSICAL IMPACT

It's now well understood that intergenerational trauma leaves lasting marks not only on our psyche, but also on our physical bodies. The Adverse Childhood Experiences study, conducted in the 1990s, surveyed people about their health history and found that trauma was associated with a profound increase in risk for a wide range of chronic diseases. Much higher rates of diabetes, obesity, depression, suicide attempts, sexually transmitted disease, heart disease, cancer, stroke, and pulmonary disease were found in those who reported traumatic events in childhood, as were higher rates of smoking, alcoholism, and drug use.

Dale has type II diabetes, and his management of the condition is so poor that his leg will likely need to be amputated if he doesn't learn to take better care of his health. In therapy, Dale identified intergenerational trauma passed on by his parents and grandparents. When Dale was a child, the adults in his life saw themselves as unworthy and less than. His grandparents were impoverished, hard-working, and "never had time" for doctors or education. His parents didn't have a lot of money, and Dale grew up eating fast food and cheap frozen dinners. Dale's parents believed in corporal punishment and beat him often; his grandparents were refugees and taught Dale to be invisible and keep his head down. Dale learned all of these lessons well and felt he had no right to ask for help; his life was so much better than his grandparents', so how could he even complain? Internalizing these messages prevented Dale from prioritizing his own health and self-care.

As seen in Dale's story, intergenerational trauma can affect our behavior in ways that put our physical health at serious risk. Unresolved trauma can also be held in our body and affect our health directly. When trauma puts us out of our window of tolerance frequently and for prolonged periods, our sympathetic nervous system, hyperarousal (see chapter 1), gets stuck in the "on" position, or, conversely, the parasympathetic nervous system, hypoarousal, gets stuck in the "off" position. And that takes a toll on our bodies. In addition, as we also discussed in chapter 1, a traumatic event can have genetic effects that are passed on from parent to child, possibly affecting the child's physical health.

Studies have found that individuals diagnosed with post-traumatic stress disorder, for example, suffer more frequently from all sorts of physical problems, including:

- Chronic fatigue

- Gastrointestinal distress

- Irritable bowel syndrome

- Autoimmune disorders

- Back pain

- Chronic pain

- Fibromyalgia

- Food allergies and environmental sensitivities

- Skin sensitivities

- Asthma

- Arthritis

- Obesity

- Diabetes

- Pulmonary diseases

- Heart problems

- Headaches

- Hypertension

- Migraines

Cody suffered from chronic back pain, but when she started therapy, its connection to her trauma wasn't clear to her. Over time, she realized that because of her relationship with an abusive father, she had developed hypervigilance—she was always on guard, had a harsh inner critic, and had extremely high expectations of herself. She was chronically constricted, both emotionally and physically. Keeping her emotions shut down, and her muscles tight and contracted, seem to be at the root of her chronic pain. Somatic therapy and dealing with her emotions, plus exercise, stretching, and relaxation techniques helped her unclench her tightened muscle fibers and experience relief.

The good news is that, as Cody's example shows, we can create healthy changes to improve and heal the impact of intergenerational trauma on our body. Increasing our window of tolerance to better manage stress and committing to self-care that keeps us strong and healthy enables us to break the grip that trauma has on our physical well-being.

First, though, we want to ease you into more awareness of physical symptoms and sensations. Thinking about your physical symptoms as being related to trauma can be triggering or bring up distressing feelings. Many of us have never thought about it in this way. It's normal to protect yourself by considering physical difficulties as a separate issue; this guards you from feeling the pain of unresolved intergenerational trauma. This next exercise will help you become more comfortable with the concept by introducing ways to connect with your body.

# AWARENESS AND RELAXATION FOR THE BODY

In this exercise you'll increase your capacity to notice symptoms and sensations in your body and learn to calm those symptoms by using your awareness to refocus on areas that feel comfortable or neutral.

1.  Begin by settling down in a comfortable position, grounding yourself. Breathe with slow belly breaths, in through your nose and out through your mouth.

2.  As you feel your breathing, imagine each indrawn breath filling your nasal passages, then moving down your throat, filling your throat with oxygen and energy. Continue to follow your breath as it settles behind your clavicle, fills your heart, moves down your midline to your belly. Feel your breath filling your abdomen.

3.  Bring your awareness as you follow your breath down through your legs into your feet. Imagine your feet grounding you and gathering more energy from the earth.

4.  Imagine your breath flowing back up along your spine, feeding oxygen to all parts of your body.

5.  Exhale, and continue to breathe slow, comfortable breaths.

6.  Focus your attention on your body. See if you can notice places of warmth and openness, and places of constriction and tightness.

7.  Where you notice discomfort or constriction, imagine feeling it with just the tip of your finger. Then, shift your attention to a spot that feels more neutral or relaxed. The relaxed place may be tiny—it could be the tip of your nose, your earlobe, the palm of your hand, or any small place that may be relaxed or neutral. Breathe, and pause with your attention at the neutral or more relaxed space.

8.  Imagine your breath flowing through your entire being. If your attention goes back to a distressed area, repeat step 7.

9.  Continue until you feel relaxed or are ready to stop. Gently return your attention to your surroundings.

Once you're familiar with the exercise, try to allow yourself the time to do a body relaxation each day. Spend 3 to 5 minutes on the exercise to start, 5 to 10 minutes once you're feeling more comfortable with it, and 15 to 30 minutes for a more advanced session.

## MIND AND BODY CONNECTION

In this exercise, from neuroaffective touch, we want to help you think about the links between your body and mind. The more you practice thinking this way, the stronger that understanding becomes and the more new neural pathways you develop. By deepening these pathways in your brain, you set yourself up to replace old maladaptive habits with new, healthy ones.

On the following page, you'll find some writing prompts designed to spark a conversation between your body and your mind. By imagining such a conversation, you'll open yourself to better communication between your mind and body.

Here's an example of how this conversation might go.

**STEP 1:** Ask your body: *Hello body, would you be willing to talk to our mind?*

**STEP 2:** If the answer is yes, ask, *Body, what would you like me to know?* What response can you imagine?

> **RESPONSE:** *I am aching and fatigued all over. Do you know any trauma reasons that I might be so uncomfortable?*

**STEP 3:** Ask for the mind's response.

> **RESPONSE:** *Yes, body, I can think of reasons you are exhausted. You have lived your life alone; there's been no one to help you. You do everything yourself; you shop alone, put away groceries alone, lift heavy boxes alone. As a child you had to do everything on your own; you played alone, you lived in fear that someone would hurt you, you held yourself small and tight to try and make yourself invisible.*

**STEP 4:** What might the body say back to that?

>**RESPONSE:** *Yes, it has been such a heavy burden to be alone and frightened. But maybe now I can ease this burden. I can use resources that I didn't have before. Maybe I can become less constricted. Maybe I can allow myself to relax sometimes.*

Now try it yourself.

**STEP 1:** Ask your body: *Hello body, would you be willing to talk to our mind?*

**STEP 2:** If the answer is no, and it feels that your body and mind are not ready to have a conversation, you can return to this exercise at a future time. If the answer is yes, ask, *Body, what would you like me to know?*

What response can you imagine?

>**RESPONSE:**

_____

_____

_____

_____

_____

**STEP 1:** Ask for the mind's response.

>**RESPONSE:**

_____

_____

_____

_____

_____

**STEP 2:** What might the body say back to that?

**RESPONSE:**

_____

_____

_____

_____

_____

When you're finished, repeat this affirmation:

*As I learn about the mind-body connection, I realize that I have the ability
to make changes that will affect my health and well-being in positive ways.
I will continue this dialogue between my mind and body. I will let my body ask
my mind, Am I safe right now? Is this fear I sense in my body from
today or from the past? If I allow myself to become more aware of what
my body needs, I can learn to treat it more kindly. I will encourage my mind
and body to work together. I now know that by healing from my trauma,
my overall health and well-being will also improve.*

# Peter

Peter came into therapy because of gastrointestinal problems and inflammation of his joints. He had been to numerous doctors, each of whom told him his problems had no medical cause and recommended seeking therapeutic support. Peter also described feelings of anxiety and doom. He suffered from panic attacks that seemed to both trigger and be triggered by his gastrointestinal symptoms. He twice thought he was having a heart attack and went to the emergency room, where he was diagnosed with panic attack and stress disorder and was told that stress was at the root of his medical problems.

Peter reported being anxious throughout his life. His issues started in high school, but even earlier than that Peter can recall feeling anxious, "scared," and often sick to his stomach. He found it difficult to make friends, because he was afraid he would have diarrhea and be found out. His father and mother seemed to have no patience for his symptoms. His father felt that if Peter was toughened up, he would grow out of it, and he often accused Peter of exaggerating or making things up. It turns out that Peter's mother had a very complicated, high-stress pregnancy because Peter's father was having an affair at the time. When Peter was born, he was very difficult to soothe and cried all the time. His mother, distraught, didn't know what to do and just let him cry. She felt angry and overwhelmed by Peter and by her husband. Peter's earliest memories are of his parents fighting; he remembers being afraid his parents might divorce and thinking that if he were a less difficult child, his parents wouldn't fight.

In therapy, Peter was able to connect his fear and anxiety to his childhood environment. With continued work, he was able to see how this fear and anxiety had fueled his physical symptoms. This helped Peter become hopeful in a way that he never had been before, because he knew there was a reason for the trauma underlying his symptoms and that he could do something to help reduce the symptoms. Peter learned how to calm his nervous system, his body, and his mind, and slowly his symptoms reduced, enabling him to feel more alive and empowered.

# FOCUS ON SELF-CARE

Now that you've learned how your body and mind are interconnected, it's important to think about how you care for your body and mind. Healing trauma means making self-care a priority.

Self-care can look different for different people. It can mean nurturing your mind and your body. It can mean noticing what you eat, improving your exercise habits, or pampering yourself. Do you get enough sleep? Do you buy yourself new clothes if you need them? Self-care can also mean setting boundaries, asking for what you need, and allowing yourself to say no.

The idea of self-care can be foreign to some or seem impossible. The quality of care and nurturing you received as a child forms the template for how you take care of yourself as you grow up. So, if your needs were not adequately met when you were young, it may be difficult for you to prioritize self-care as an adult. In addition, unresolved trauma may keep you from being aware of what you need, want, or feel.

For some, it may be easier to take care of others and ignore or neglect one's own self-care. In that case, it's good to recall the instructions that flight attendants give: In an emergency, put on your own oxygen mask first. Then, you can help someone else put on theirs.

An important tool for improving self-care is a *routine*. For many trauma survivors, self-care is last on their list of priorities, if it makes the list at all. When there's a choice between self-care and some other activity, self-care loses every time. But building self-care into your schedule—making it a routine—removes any need to make a decision. Over time, a healthy habit becomes established and replaces older, maladaptive patterns.

Julie was on a path of recovery from alcoholism and had been sober for two weeks. She got into a fight with her boyfriend, and the first thing she did was drink. Drinking as a soothing response to conflict was still second nature for her. After maintaining sobriety for five months, following a 12-step program that included attending daily meetings, Julie again had a fight with her boyfriend. This time, instead of drinking, she practiced self-care, called her sponsor and went to a meeting. Julie found that by attending meetings regularly and talking daily with her sponsor, she was able to make self-care part of her life in a way she'd never done before.

Self-care routines and habits can be very soothing; they create predictability and clear expectations. Our body responds to what it knows is going to happen, so routines of self-care can help calm the body's fear of danger. Instead of expecting deprivation or lack of attention, your body learns to expect care, compassion, soothing, and fun. Self-care sends a message to the self: I am worthy. I am lovable. I deserve to be cared for. The more we give ourselves these messages, the more we begin to really internalize and believe them. Our self-esteem grows. Our self-image becomes more positive.

# HOW DO I CARE FOR MYSELF?

If you listen to your body, it has a lot to tell you. When you talk to your body and it says, "I need some nourishment, I need some love, I need some space, I need a walk, I need some warmth," then you have ideas of what to do to take care of yourself. In the previous exercise, you imagined a literal conversation with your body. This time, you're going to answer some questions about how you take care of your body, in order to establish self-care goals and routines.

Answer the following questions as accurately as you can, estimating the numbers if necessary.

How much sleep do you get a night?

_____

_____

_____

How often do you exercise each week?

_____

_____

_____

Do you eat healthfully? What foods make up most of your diet?

_____

_____

_____

_____

How do you care for your body?

_____

_____

_____

_____

How often do you pamper yourself? In what ways?

_____

_____

_____

_____

Do you ever take "me time"? What does that look like?

_____

_____

_____

_____

What kind of emotional support do you have: friends, support groups, therapy, other?

_____

_____

_____

_____

What do you do for fun?

_____

_____

_____

_____

How do you set boundaries, to make sure you have time for yourself?

_____

_____

_____

_____

What interferes with the time you reserve for yourself?

_____

_____

_____

_____

What are some activities that give you pleasure?

_____

_____

_____

_____

Are you doing these activities frequently? If not, why not?

_____

_____

_____

_____

What feeds your soul?

_____

_____

_____

_____

When you're finished, pause to reflect. Ask yourself: _How would I treat myself, what would I do for myself, if I loved myself more?_

If that's too difficult to answer, then imagine yourself as a child. How would the adult you care for that child?

If your answers aren't positive, you may need therapeutic support to help develop a more compassionate relationship with yourself.

In this exercise, you'll create two charts: one to illustrate how you're currently spending your time, and another to illustrate how your time could be better managed to make room for self-care.

Review the sample pie chart, which displays the daily activity of someone who's not making self-care a priority.

Then, use the first blank pie chart to document your own activity on a typical day. Each of the segments represents one hour of time; determine how much time you spend on each activity, and fill in the pie chart accordingly (round up to the nearest hour). You can label the segments, fill them in with different colors, or designate them however you wish.

Activities to include on the chart:

- Sleeping

- Working

- Socializing

- General self-care

- Exercise

- Taking care of obligations

- Relaxing

- Having fun

- Family time

- Chores

- Television or screen time

- Caring for others

- Checking out

Add your own

- _____

- _____

## SAMPLE PIE CHART

How I spend my time:                              How I'd like to spend my time:

How much time, in a typical day, do you spend doing things that are good for your health? For many trauma survivors, the first pie chart will be unbalanced: heavy on work and responsibilities, and light on socializing, relaxing, and fun. Review your chart, then draw a second chart that represents how you'd like to spend your time, with a life more in balance. What activities do you need to prioritize or limit?

As you look at your charts, think about what you need to do in order to move toward an ideal, more balanced use of time. What changes do you need to make? What feelings do you notice in your body as you imagine living a life more in line with your ideal?

On the lines below, write about the activities that you would like to increase and decrease in order to create a healthier, more balanced use of your time.

_____

_____

_____

_____

_____

# VISUALIZING SELF-CARE

In this exercise, you'll use all of your senses to imagine yourself doing a self-care activity that has brought joy or comfort in the past. The purposes of this visualization are to help deepen your appreciation of self-care and to give you a resource to use whenever you need to connect with calming, positive feelings. In addition, when you actually do a self-care activity, this exercise will help you notice more deeply the good feelings.

1. Sit in a comfortable position. Notice your breath and feel your feet on the ground.

2. Close your eyes, or focus on a spot in the room if you prefer to keep them open.

3. Bring into your mind's eye a snapshot of yourself participating in a healthy self-care activity. It can be anything that's beneficial for your mind or body—a physical activity, a hobby that relaxes you, or a pampering treatment like a massage or pedicure.

4. Engage all your senses to experience the imaginary activity. Notice all the colors and shapes, whatever you may smell, any textures or tactile sensations, sounds, your gut reaction, and any emotions that arise. For example, if your activity is baking cookies, imagine the feeling of the dough under your fingers, the smell of the kitchen, the taste of a freshly baked cookie, and the feeling of pleasure and satisfaction as you set them out to cool. If your activity is gardening, imagine having your fingers in the dirt, planting the seeds, pulling weeds, feeling the sun on your face, the smell of the soil and flowers, and the feelings of appreciation for nature and being proud of your garden bed.

5. Take as much time as you like to sit with these sensations. When you're ready, slowly bring your attention back to your surroundings.

Afterward, take some time for reflection. What was it like to practice these activities in your mind? What sensations did you notice in your body as you imagined this self-care activity? Did you notice a change in your breath, your posture? Did you notice a change in your mood, a calmness, a sense of contentment, as you imagined doing your activity? Did your body calm or soften? Or was there no change?

If your experience was positive, this is a great resource for you. You can perform the imaginary activity whenever you don't have time or opportunity for the real thing.

If it was a negative experience, that's okay; the goal is to find another activity that feels more positive for you. You might have to experiment with a few different imaginary activities, or try new ones that you haven't previously engaged in.

# SELF-CARE EVERY DAY

As you come to understand the connection between your mind and body more deeply, and how trauma affects your health and well-being, every day is an opportunity to rethink how you care for your body and yourself.

To help expand your thinking, here are some ideas for self-care activities. Please feel free to add your own:

- Mindfulness
- Meditation
- Hobbies
- Sleep
- Healthy eating
- Exercise
- Yoga
- Breathwork
- Baths
- Swimming
- Heating pads
- Candles
- Aromatherapy (lavender in particular)
- Gardening
- Being outdoors
- Hiking
- Visiting the ocean
- Coloring
- Knitting

- Walking
- Drumming
- Cooking or baking
- Self-pampering
- Listening to or playing music
- Massage
- Social connections
- Reading
- Learning
- Dance
- Movement
- Spiritual practices
- Self-help groups
- Therapy
- Spending time with pets
- Volunteering or being of service to others
- Being with loved ones

# OWNING YOUR SELF-CARE

In this exercise, we want to help you create your go-to self-care list. Making your decisions explicit by writing them out helps make you more accountable to yourself, which in turn helps you follow through.

Use the table on page 120 to list the ways in which you take care of yourself. Write how often you are currently doing each of these activities, and how you'd like to increase these activities in the future. Review the example below, then move on to create a list of activities you currently do, the frequency, your goal frequency, and some that you'd like to try in the future.

| CURRENT ACTIVITY | CURRENT FREQUENCY | GOAL FREQUENCY |
|---|---|---|
| Gardening | Once a month | Weekends |
| Listening to music | When driving to and from work | When driving; evenings at home |
| Meditation | 10 minutes once a week | 15 minutes four times a week |
| Socializing with friends | Every few months | Once a week |

| CURRENT ACTIVITY | CURRENT FREQUENCY | GOAL FREQUENCY |
| --- | --- | --- |
| | | |
| | | |
| | | |
| | | |
| | | |
| | | |

| FUTURE ACTIVITY | INTENDED FREQUENCY |
| --- | --- |
| | |

Take a moment to reflect. Looking at your table, notice what comes up for you. Does it feel like enough, or not enough? How do you feel about the idea of increasing your self-care? When adding new activities, don't worry about finding the time—just add anything you might enjoy. Go wild!

## MOTIVATION AND FOLLOW-THROUGH

What interferes with your self-care? Thinking about this will prepare you to challenge some of the obstacles and strategize ways to succeed or motivate yourself.

What are the family messages that might interfere with following through on self-care?

_____

_____

_____

_____

_____

How can you challenge these beliefs?

_____

_____

_____

_____

_____

What are the cultural messages that might interfere with following through on self-care?

_____

_____

_____

_____

How would you challenge these beliefs?

_____

_____

_____

_____

What negative messages do you tell yourself about the value of self-care?

_____

_____

_____

_____

What would be more helpful to tell yourself?

_____

_____

_____

_____

What else do you imagine will interfere with practicing more self-care?

_____

_____

_____

_____

What can you do to decrease interference?

_____

_____

_____

_____

What are your priorities; what is most important to you? Work, health, family, or something else?

_____

_____

_____

_____

Are there shifts you'd like to make in your priorities? Does the way you spend your time match with what you believe is important to you?

_____

_____

_____

_____

What new beliefs or self-talk will help you self-motivate?

_____

_____

_____

_____

How do you imagine your life can change with better self-care?

_____

_____

_____

_____

As a next step, try to tell yourself this each morning: *I will do my best to put myself at the top of my to-do list each day.*

Each night, tell yourself: *I did my best today, tomorrow is another day.*

It's important to remember that part of self-care will be to not judge or criticize yourself, but rather to remind yourself that building new habits and giving yourself permission to take care of yourself can be harder than it sounds.

## YOUR ACTIVITY TRACKER

Now that you have explored self-care, you may have noticed ways in which you are, and are not, taking care of yourself. Empowered by that knowledge, you're ready to set goals and schedule your self-care, making it a more permanent part of your routine. Seeing the activity on your calendar may even help give you permission to take this time for yourself. And, from a practical standpoint, designating time for self-care can help support a move toward a more balanced, healthier lifestyle.

Drawing from your pie chart (page 115) and self-care activity list (page 120), fill in the following weekly calendars. Try to give yourself at least one self-care goal per day, even something as simple as five to ten minutes of meditation, or getting to bed at a reasonable bedtime.

For each activity, follow these steps:

**STEP 1:** Set a time-related goal for the activity. Challenge yourself, but err on the side of being realistic. You can change the goal if it turns out to be too difficult.

> **Examples:** *I will exercise for at least 45 minutes, 3 times a week. I will see a movie with friends once a month.*

**STEP 2:** Decide where you want to place the goal on your schedule, and write it on the Week One calendar.

**STEP 3:** If there are steps you need to take before you can achieve this goal, set goals for them, too.

> **Examples:** *I would like to have new running shoes by next week. I will call friends today to set up a movie date.*

Enter your goals on the calendar. If your original goal is pushed back because you have preliminary goals to accomplish, then adjust accordingly.

**STEP 4:** Repeat for each self-care activity you would like to include in your routine.

**STEP 5:** Fill in the Week Two, Three, and Four calendars. You can repeat the same schedule or increase the frequency if it seems appropriate. Alternately, just fill in Week Two, then reevaluate the following weeks after you've tried out your new schedule.

## SAMPLE CALENDAR

| TIME | MON | TUE | WED | THU | FRI | SAT | SUN |
|------|-----|-----|-----|-----|-----|-----|-----|
| 7:00–9:00 a.m. | Exercise | Meditation | Exercise | Meditation | Exercise | Buy new running shoes | Meditation |
| 9:00 a.m.–5:00 p.m. | Work | Work | Work | Work | Work | Self-reflection | Hiking |
| 5:00–7:00 p.m. | Evening with friends | Family time | Errands | Family time | Knitting class, family dinner (take-out) | Errands | Free time at park |
| 7:00–9:00 p.m. | Time with kids, homework or TV or games | Call friends to set movie date or socialize | Play time with kids | Read or play Words with Friends | Aromatherapy bath, read books with kids | Date night with husband | Reading time |
| 10:00–11:00 p.m. | Quiet time | Quiet time | Bath time | Self-pampering | Puzzle time | Music time | Quiet time |
| 11:00 p.m. | Bedtime | Bedtime | Bedtime | Free time | Free time | Free time | Bedtime |

Now it's your turn.

## WEEK ONE

| TIME | MON | TUE | WED | THU | FRI | SAT | SUN |
|------|-----|-----|-----|-----|-----|-----|-----|
|      |     |     |     |     |     |     |     |

## WEEK TWO

| TIME | MON | TUE | WED | THU | FRI | SAT | SUN |
|------|-----|-----|-----|-----|-----|-----|-----|
|      |     |     |     |     |     |     |     |

# WEEK THREE

| TIME | MON | TUE | WED | THU | FRI | SAT | SUN |
|------|-----|-----|-----|-----|-----|-----|-----|
|      |     |     |     |     |     |     |     |

## WEEK FOUR

| TIME | MON | TUE | WED | THU | FRI | SAT | SUN |
|------|-----|-----|-----|-----|-----|-----|-----|
|      |     |     |     |     |     |     |     |
|      |     |     |     |     |     |     |     |

We strongly suggest starting your day with a quiet moment of reflection or meditation to set the tone for the rest of your day.

Notice after a week, or a month, what has changed in your life. What self-talk did you use to push past any interference or avoidance? How is your self-care making a difference?

If you have struggled to meet your daily goals, be gentle with yourself; hopefully, you have been able to create a schedule; that is a great beginning!

# CHAPTER HIGHLIGHTS

- Unresolved intergenerational trauma can affect our physical, as well as emotional and mental, health.

- Our body and mind interact and affect each other.

- Trauma and PTSD increase the occurrence of physical disease.

- We can change discomfort in the body by noticing areas of physical distress and shifting attention to calmer areas.

- Allowing our mind and body to dialogue together can help us better know our needs.

- Improving our health is possible with a focus on self-care. Making self-care a priority is crucial for healthy living.

- Routines and scheduling can help us follow through and be accountable to our needs.

- Gentleness to self is an important self-care activity.

# CHAPTER 6

# HEALING YOUR RELATIONSHIPS

All of our current relationships are based on our earliest relationships, starting from the interactions we had with our primary caretakers. The people taking care of us when we were first born. Those experiences form a model of how relationships work that we carry throughout our lives. For those of us who've experienced intergenerational trauma, it's a maladaptive model, a broken template that has a detrimental impact on our ability to form and maintain healthy relationships. In this chapter we're going to deepen your understanding of the ways that trauma affects attachment styles. We'll discuss protective strategies that may be sabotaging your connections with the people in your life, and we'll explore healthier ways to cope with communication and boundary issues. Lastly, we'll focus on the importance of self-love as a foundation for healthy relationships.

# UNDERSTANDING RELATIONSHIP ISSUES

We often find ourselves choosing partners that feel like home. And if our personal history includes intergenerational trauma, that can mean we unconsciously mesh with others who either replicate our past trauma or fill the deficits that trauma has left behind.

Melanie's father struggled with alcoholism. At age 40, Melanie found that her spouse had a substance abuse disorder. She came to therapy because she wanted to understand how to better help her husband. She said that she loved him and that their relationship would be perfect if he could just quit drinking. Melanie believed that she couldn't live without him and was desperate for a solution. She spent much of her time and energy focused on keeping the latest addiction-related crisis under control, and felt like a failure when she couldn't. In therapy, Melanie came to realize that these were similar to the feelings she'd had about her father. As a child, she'd believed that his bad behavior was somehow her fault and that she needed to find a way to fix it.

Following a model that's distorted by intergenerational trauma, you may find yourself in the same type of relationship over and over again and wonder why nothing changes. You might feel hopeless and give up on trying to find a partner, or resign yourself to an unhealthy relationship, thinking this is as good as it gets. You may blame yourself when a relationship is failing or increase your efforts to change the other person. If you have children, you may find yourself parenting in the same way that your parents did, or doing the polar opposite, based on your primary caretaker's way of nurturing.

The quality of our early relationships enables us to form what's described as an *attachment style*—our primary way of interacting and behaving with other people. If we were nurtured, attuned to, and made to feel safe throughout our earliest development, we will likely go on to have a secure attachment style. If this didn't happen, our connection style will more likely be insecure. An insecure attachment style typically features protective strategies that we've learned to keep us feeling safe. The earlier in our lives that trauma or abuse occurs, the more deeply it affects our ability to connect to ourselves, others, or to our own needs.

There are four primary attachment styles in adults.

| ATTACHMENT STYLE | CHARACTERIZED BY | PARENT WAS LIKELY |
|---|---|---|
| Secure | • Good self-esteem<br><br>• Ability to be one's authentic self<br><br>• Feeling safe with others and in the world<br><br>• Low anxiety<br><br>• Ability to take appropriate risks<br><br>• Awareness of one's own needs<br><br>• Willingness to ask for needs to be met<br><br>• Flexibility regarding self, others, conflict resolution, and life challenges<br><br>• Healthy communication style<br><br>• Ability to live with joy in the world<br><br>• Ability to deal with disappointments and failure as well as embrace success | • Nurturing and highly attuned to the child's needs |
| Dismissive-Avoidant (insecure) | • Emotional distance or unavailability<br><br>• Tendency to reject others<br><br>• Difficulty developing or maintaining close connections to others<br><br>• Difficulty knowing one's own feelings<br><br>• Difficulty knowing or expressing needs<br><br>• Difficulty sharing personal feelings with others, high value on independence and privacy<br><br>• Strict boundaries<br><br>• Avoidance of emotional intimacy in relationships or dealing with problems in relationships | • Emotionally unavailable or rejecting |

*Table continues* ⟶

| ATTACHMENT STYLE | CHARACTERIZED BY | PARENT WAS LIKELY |
|---|---|---|
| Anxious-Preoccupied (insecure) | • Need for constant reassurance in relationships<br>• High levels of insecurity<br>• Fear of rejection<br>• Distrust of others<br>• Need for validation<br>• Codependence<br>• Preoccupation with the relationship<br>• Clingy behavior<br>• Poor personal boundaries<br>• Controlling behavior; inability to self-regulate<br>• Difficulty identifying one's own needs | • Emotionally dysregulated or intrusive<br>• Not attuned to the child's needs |
| Fearful-Avoidant (insecure) | • Negative view of self and others<br>• Feeling unsafe in the world<br>• Confusion regarding feelings and relationships<br>• Confliction over wanting to be close and wanting to pull away<br>• Unpredictable behavior<br>• Vacillation between aggressive and affectionate behavior<br>• Depression and anxiety<br>• Emotional outbursts | • Frightened or frightening to the child<br>• Abusive or extremely neglectful |

The four attachment styles are reflected in the way we connect to others. We may predominantly use one style or deploy more than one. For example, a person in a 12-step group may have a secure attachment to their sponsor, but an insecure attachment to their spouse or romantic partner. The good news is that your attachment style can change as you heal.

Laura was a 35-year-old woman having difficulty in relationships. She said she wanted to marry and have children. She had a serious relationship when she was 25, but it ended because he drifted away and may have been cheating. Laura had many suitors since, but always lost interest. She became most interested in men who were unavailable, married, or preoccupied with their careers. Laura shared that she'd had a very depressed mother and a father who worked all the time. Therapy helped her become aware of her avoidant attachment style and how it protected her from true intimacy, which was extremely frightening to her, even though she also longed for it.

Insecure attachments depend on protective strategies that address the fears and insecurities that can be produced by intergenerational trauma. Some common protective strategies include:

**AVOIDING RELATIONSHIPS.** You steer clear of relationships altogether or enter a relationship with someone who isn't available. Since there's no true relationship, your fear of abandonment or rejection is eased.

**RESISTING CONNECTIONS TO OTHERS.** You find it difficult to trust others and have fears of intimacy and closeness. You find yourself sabotaging relationships by questioning the other person's integrity, finding fault, or pulling away so you don't have to face your fear.

**CLINGINESS.** You make excessive demands for time and attention. You may feel like you never get enough of the other person, and you constantly ask for reassurance.

**CODEPENDENCY.** You care more for others than for yourself, putting their needs before your own and not feeling okay if they don't feel okay. You may seek validation, basing your self-worth on how others treat you.

**DISTRUST.** You feel unable to fully trust anyone and keep a wall between yourself and others. You may never fully share feelings, and you may be suspicious of others.

**LOW SELF-ESTEEM.** You don't believe in yourself and rely on others to make decisions, giving you a false sense of security.

**CONTROL.** You may find the need to constantly be in control of everything, in order to manage your anxiety in relationships and manage your levels of closeness and distance.

The next exercises are designed to help you identify your current attachment patterns, find the roots of them in your family history, and begin working toward a more secure attachment style.

# ATTACHMENT STYLES SYMPTOM CHECKLIST

Identifying your predominant attachment style—or combination of styles—is a necessary step toward being able to challenge and change them.

Review the attachment styles chart on page 135 and circle the qualities that seem most representative of how you experience relationships. Remember that you may relate to more than one category, but generally we each have a predominant style. It may be helpful to think about one important relationship during this process, preferably with a romantic partner or parent.

Next, informed by the qualities you identified, respond to the prompts below.

Upon reflecting on the four attachment categories, I think I fall in the category of

_____ most often.

I know this because of these attachment behaviors:

_____

_____

_____

Do you feel that you self-regulate (self-soothe) well, or do you respond better to co-regulation (being soothed by others)?

_____

_____

Explain the ways in which you self-regulate and/or co-regulate (manage your mood) by interacting with others.

_____

_____

What are some changes you would need to see in yourself to allow for secure attachment relationships?

_____

_____

_____

_____

How would your current relationship be different if you were more securely attached?

_____

_____

_____

_____

When you've completed the exercise, take a moment and repeat this affirmation to yourself:

> *In order to securely attach, I must experience some of what was missing in my childhood. I can begin this by focusing on healthy relationships that I do have, or I can imagine parenting my inner child in a loving and nurturing way.*

Imagine that your younger self is sitting on your knee. What are some of the nurturing things that you could say to the child version of you? Learning to love the wounded child inside you can increase your ability to securely attach to yourself and to others. If you can't imagine loving yourself, try to imagine the love you have for a child or a pet, or the love you've seen someone else express toward their child.

# REFLECTIONS ON YOUR INTERGENERATIONAL ATTACHMENT ROOTS

Now, we'd like you to explore the way that attachment styles are transmitted from generation to generation. This will help you better uncouple the past from the present, on your way to developing more secure attachments.

Answer the questions below.

When thinking about your relationships with your primary caregivers as a child, do you feel that you were securely or insecurely attached to them? Explain why.

_____

_____

_____

_____

_____

How would you characterize your parents' attachment to each other? Share examples.

_____

_____

_____

_____

_____

Can you trace any attachment patterns in the relationships between your grandparents and your parents? What behaviors can you identify that have been passed on from one generation to the next? Go as far back as you can, or want to, in your family tree. Give examples that illustrate these intergenerational patterns.

_____

_____

_____

_____

_____

_____

How did trauma influence these attachment patterns? What events are you aware of that may have had an impact?

_____

_____

_____

_____

_____

_____

When you've completed the exercise, take a moment and ask yourself: *How does this exploration of intergenerational trauma help unchain me from the past*? For example, does it change your sense of your family? Does it help you have more compassion for yourself or them? Seeing how your patterns of attachment are rooted in the past, try repeating this statement:

*I am influenced by the past, but I can change in the present.*

# Tracey

Tracey came into therapy to combat her depression, inability to feel truly connected to anyone, and worry about how this lack of deep connection will affect her children. As Tracey's story unfolded, it was evident that her mother, Anne, had suffered with depression and low self-esteem and depended on her husband Bob to take care of everything. Bob's mother had a mental illness, so it seemed natural for him to be a caretaker. But, eventually, he burned out and divorced Tracey's mother, Anne. When he left, Anne became more severely depressed and stayed in bed all day, to the point that her children feared she would kill herself. Tracey and her siblings had to take care of their mother, and, due to her fragility, they were afraid to bother her with their needs. Tracey ended up feeling like the parent to her siblings.

As Tracey explored her intergenerational roots, she found out that her maternal grandfather had died when her mother was a child. Her grandmother, who had no education and no career path, was forced to leave her children for long hours to clean other people's houses for money. Tracey's grandmother had no time for the kids' feelings; there was no coddling in her house. But there was also no mention of love. Tracey's mother said she never heard her mother say, "I love you." In therapy, Tracey began to challenge her inability to connect, which meant challenging her vulnerability. She learned to pause and be in the moment, and to separate her childhood idea of love and her adult sense of love. She recognized that she was avoiding emotions, and through therapy she worked on expanding her capacity to feel. For Tracey, healing was a long journey of returning to parts of herself that she had kept locked away.

## SELF-LOVE LETTER

Now that you've identified your attachment style, considered how it affects your relationships, and envisioned how your relationships could be improved with a different style of attachment, it's time to express those thoughts in a letter to yourself.

Write your letter in the space below or on a separate sheet of paper. Write freely, and try to include the following:

- Some ways in which you'd like to be more compassionate to yourself.

- Statements you would have liked to have heard when you were a child.

- A description of how you'd like to be treated in a relationship, and how you would like to treat others.

- Words of forgiveness for what feel like poor choices you've made, or for carrying on the insecure attachment patterns you learned as a child into your adult relationships with children, partners, and others.

### DEAR ME,

_____

_____

_____

_____

_____

_____

_____

_____

_____

_____

_____

_____

_____

_____

_____

_____

_____

Reread your letter often, asking yourself: *Am I loving myself the way that I hoped I would? Am I loving others the way that I hoped I would?*

# THE ROLE OF COMMUNICATION

Healthy communication is key to healthy relationships. But healthy communication is about more than the spoken word: It has everything to do with our perception of what's being communicated, and how we are primed to react to communication from others. Our attachment styles and our family history greatly influence the healthy or not-so-healthy ways that we communicate. Families can have unspoken rules about what can or cannot be talked about. There may be little language for emotional expression. Asking about needs may be discouraged or not permitted.

When Donny was an infant, no one came when he cried, so he stopped crying to express his needs. But he also stopped communicating his feelings altogether. He learned to push them down, disconnecting from his emotions and needs so much that even as an adult he wasn't consciously aware of them. He came to therapy because of ongoing problems in his marriage. He found himself angry with his partner for not knowing his needs, and his anger came out toward his husband in passive but aggressive communication. Rather than saying what was wrong, Donny would slam doors, leave the house, or make snide remarks about something that wasn't the actual problem. Lacking the ability to ask for what he wanted, Donny essentially expected his partner to read his mind, an impossibility that was bound to cause difficulties in the relationship.

The interactions between trauma and communication can be complicated. In some families, language itself can be traumatizing, used to emotionally control or abuse family members. In others, trauma is expressed through overexpression of emotions: yelling, hysteria, or constant demand for co-regulation ("fix me," "make me feel better," "solve my problems"). Children may grow up emulating dysfunctional ways of communicating, or they may learn to hide or carefully monitor the way that they communicate in order to not make waves.

Joely had been a screamer in her communications with her children. She had not learned how to regulate her feelings and found herself feeling out of control. Wanting to change this pattern, she talked to her children about how her own parents always screamed when they were having large feelings, and how yelling in her family had been a normal way of communicating. She pointed out to her children that they too yelled. By learning to regulate herself, Joely was able to help her children learn to manage their emotions. She taught them to pause when they were feeling big feelings. Together as a family, they learned to communicate more calmly.

Having the ability to know and understand our own internal messages and triggers is an important component of effective communication with others. This self-communication includes listening to your feelings, core beliefs, and the sensations of your body. Learning to listen to yourself can help you regulate your mood and emotions before communicating.

It's also important to keep aware of your internal signals during communication with others. This means learning to uncouple the past and hearing your communicating with your partner based on the present. Check in with yourself about what your partner is saying versus what you are hearing. What do you sense in your body? Are you enjoying the interaction? Are you feeling safe, anxious, or nervous? The clues that your body shares with you can keep you authentic, because body language is also a form of communication. Your body also communicates to others what you are feeling. Do you hold yourself in a hunched posture, arms and legs crossed or tight together, or are you in an open stance, arms wide and gesturing freely? Which posture matches the feelings you're trying to express?

Georgia would become angry anytime her husband wanted to spend an evening with friends. She would lash out and accuse him of not spending enough time with her, and question whether he even cared about her at all. Her husband insisted that he loved her deeply and enjoyed spending time with her, but he said that her accusations were making him feel increasingly distant. In therapy, Georgia learned to listen to her internal messages, and she realized that her anger was rooted in a fear of abandonment—and that the fear was a reaction to her past. She learned to recognize these feelings and share them honestly with her husband rather than lashing out.

You might need to challenge yourself to ask questions, speak about things that may have been off-limits, or acknowledge your emotions in unfamiliar ways. You might also need to learn to listen in a new way so you can respond rather than react. Bringing family secrets to light may feel threatening to the connections we currently hold. And when the doors of communication have been closed for so long, it can feel "wrong" or terrifying to communicate honestly. It will be helpful to think about the boundaries that have been established and whether they are healthy or unhealthy. You can take baby steps. Here are some basic rules of good communication that may help.

**KNOW YOUR GOAL.** Before you start, think about what you want to communicate and achieve in a conversation or discussion. Try to stay focused and not bring a whole list of other issues.

**ASK FOR THE TIME.** Timing is important if you want to be heard. You may have something important to talk about, but it may not be the right time for your partner. Check with them before trying to start a substantial conversation.

**SPEAK FOR YOURSELF.** Try to stick with "I" statements ("I feel abandoned when I don't hear back from you on the same day.") and talk about yourself and your feelings. Don't put words into someone else's mouth or make assumptions about the intentions of others.

**HEAR WHAT THEY'RE SAYING.** When it's your turn to listen, try to listen openly, without judgment. Don't think about your response while the other person is talking. Ask questions or rephrase what the person said to make sure you understand.

**SIGNAL YOUR ATTENTION.** Let them know you're paying attention through nonverbal communications like making eye contact, nodding your head, making affirming sounds ("right," "mmm-hmmm"), and keeping your body turned toward them.

**PAY ATTENTION TO YOURSELF.** Notice your body's cues. Are you starting to get triggered? What are you sensing inside? If you're starting to feel uncomfortable or emotionally dysregulated, it's time to take a break.

**ERR AND REPAIR.** We all make mistakes, and communication mistakes can cause ruptures (breaks in the relationship). The important thing is to repair the rupture by identifying your miscommunication or emotional outburst or lack of attunement, and then trying to correct it.

**EXPLAIN WHAT YOU'RE THINKING.** To whatever degree is appropriate, share with your partner the meaning that you are giving to your feelings ("That makes me uncomfortable."), the meaning you are giving to a problem ("That's difficult for me to hear; it makes me feel anxious."), or the meaning you are giving to the other's communication ("I'm very sorry to hear about that.").

Improving communication in your relationships has to start with you; learning to be attuned to yourself is key. As you begin to communicate with your family about intergenerational trauma, proceed with caution. It's not always advisable to address family trauma with others, until you're ready to deal with their reactions. And there may be relationships that are so toxic or abusive that it could be unsafe to approach the person at all. Each circumstance is different, and you have to evaluate the level of safety, remembering to take care of yourself first.

With that in mind, let's move forward with some exercises designed to help you develop healthier and more productive communication.

# MY FAMILY'S COMMUNICATION STYLE

Breaking the patterns of unhealthy communication passed down through family trauma must start with knowing why you communicate the way you do. Then, you can make different choices for healthier ways of communication. In this exercise, we'll help you examine your current boundaries and communication patterns and consider ways that you can change those patterns. Please answer the following questions.

When thinking about family communication when you were growing up, in what ways did it feel healthy or unhealthy?

What topics were off-limits or avoided?

What spoken or unspoken rules were there about communication?

Growing up, were the boundaries in your family closed, tight, open, porous, or unfiltered? Describe them.

_____

_____

_____

_____

How did your family deal with conflict? What was the communication like around conflict?

_____

_____

_____

_____

How did your family communicate love? (Or did it?)

_____

_____

_____

_____

What would you like to change about the way you communicate?

_____

_____

_____

_____

What might you want to be honest about now that you weren't able to be honest about in the past?

_____

_____

_____

_____

Are there other things you'd like to see change in your family's current communication style?

_____

_____

_____

_____

What do you imagine might interfere with changing communication in the family?

_____

_____

_____

_____

When you're finished, pause to reflect. Imagine a more authentic way of communicating with your family, and how that can improve and create healthier relationships. What do you notice when you imagine this? Do you feel freer, or do you feel scared or defensive? Changing communication can be challenging for many reasons. As we begin to know our patterns, free ourselves from the past, and recognize ways we'd like to change, we must also be compassionate and patient with ourselves. Remember, you are a work in progress!

# RELATIONALLY MINDFUL COMMUNICATION

In this exercise, you'll imagine both a pleasant and an unpleasant communication experience. You'll practice focusing your attention on what was going on, bringing mindfulness to the conversation. Being mindful when communicating means reacting to the present moment and staying aware of what you're sensing, feeling, and thinking. This can help you stay in your window of tolerance and more accurately perceive what is happening in the moment. It also means being aware of triggers so your responses will be uncoupled from the past.

Imagine a recent or not-so-recent conversation that didn't go the way you wanted. (For practice, try to select something only mildly unpleasant.)

Take a moment to place yourself in the situation again, seeing and hearing the sights and sounds. As you imagine this conversation, what do you notice about yourself? What sensations do you feel in your body? What emotions come up for you as you imagine the scenario? What was your communication with the other person like? What was it about the communication that felt safe or unsafe, pleasant or unpleasant? What patterns do you notice when you think of other conversations you've had?

_____

_____

_____

_____

_____

Next, imagine a conversation that felt pleasant. If you don't have a memory to work from, imagine a pleasant conversation that you would like to have.

As you imagine this interaction, what sensations do you notice? What contributed to this being a pleasant experience? What emotions did you feel? What were your patterns of communication? Was it the topic of conversation or the person that you conversed with that made it pleasant?

---

As a next step, see if you can be mindful in your interaction with others. When you find yourself in a conversation with someone, focus your attention on what's happening in the moment. Let everything else—worries about your day, plans for lunch, speculation about what you or the other person will say next—fall away. Hear what the other person is saying, feel whatever sensations are present in your body, and notice what emotions may come up.

## TESTING THE WATER

Imagining how you would like to communicate in a relationship is a great way to move forward. A good approach to discussing a challenging subject with someone is to speak about yourself and your feelings, rather than accusing the other person or focusing on their behavior. Practicing how you want to say something difficult can be helpful.

Review the basic rules of good communication from earlier in this chapter. With those in mind, write short scripts for the scenarios listed below. You can follow the format provided, or you can write your script in your own style. Use the examples as a guide, and remember to stick to describing your feelings and suggesting what you would like to see changed.

## SCENARIO: DISCUSSING A PROBLEM IN A RELATIONSHIP

**Example script:**

*When I don't hear from you when you say you're going to call*

*I feel like you don't love me, like I'm not important to you, like you are going to leave me.*

*I would like it if you could at least send me a brief text that you're not able to call.*

### MY SCRIPT:

When I _____

I feel _____

I would like _____

## SCENARIO: MAKING SURE YOU UNDERSTAND WHAT YOUR PARTNER IS TRYING TO SAY

**Example script:**

*When I hear you say that you're bored*

*What I hear is that you're bored with me*

*Is that accurate?*

### MY SCRIPT:

When I hear you say _____

What I hear is _____

Is that accurate?

# SCENARIO: DISCUSSING UNMET NEEDS

**Example script:**

*When I am upset, I need comforting.*

*I would like to be held.*

*Is that something you can do? If not, what else might you do to help me feel comforted?*

## MY SCRIPT:

When I am _____

I would like _____

Is that something you can do? If not, what else might you do to help me feel comforted?

# SCENARIO: REQUESTING A HEART-TO-HEART CONVERSATION

**Example script:**

*Is this a good time to talk? I have something I want to discuss that might take a few minutes.*

*If not now, when might be a good time? Can we schedule a time?*

## MY SCRIPT:

Is this a good time to talk? _____

If not now, _____

As you consider these scenarios, which ones do you imagine being easiest and most difficult to navigate?

As you communicate in situations like this in your day-to-day life, it will help to first remind yourself of healthy communication rules and be aware of your triggers. And it's always a good idea to take a few moments to ground yourself with some deep breathing and meditation, if possible, before engaging in an important communication.

# CHAPTER HIGHLIGHTS

- Healthy communication is a key to healthy relationships.

- Communication patterns can be passed down intergenerationally.

- Unhealthy communication patterns develop out of our protective strategies.

- Nonverbal communication is conveyed through bodily based sensations, posture, facial expressions, and tone of voice.

- Effective verbal communication includes talking and listening skills.

- Improving communication in your relationships has to start with you.

- Healthy communication often takes planning, knowing what you want to achieve in the communication, and knowing if the time is right.

CHAPTER 7

# A NEW CYCLE BEGINS

We've reached the final chapter of this workbook, but we hope that this is only the beginning of your continued growth and healing. Now that you may be experiencing some relief, we encourage you to keep growing toward an even more expanded aliveness, connection, and joy.

Because the journey doesn't end here, this chapter will present some additional ways to move through challenges and offer some ideas for added support. We'll ask you to reflect on what you've learned about yourself, your family, and the effects of intergenerational trauma.

First, a few words about the road ahead. By now, you've spent some time imagining how you'd like to be living your life in the future, and you're equipped with some exercises and tools to help you get there. There may be times when you feel discouraged, but every road has some roadblocks and bumps. That doesn't take away from the distance you've already traveled.

# MOVING FORWARD

Healing from intergenerational trauma is not just about reducing our symptoms. It's also a path toward being present in the world in a larger way. Healing allows us to have more meaningful connections with others and with ourselves and deepens our capacity to experience all of our feelings. Remember that trauma often leads us to restrict our negative feelings, which also reduces our capacity to feel positive ones. As you expand your window of tolerance, you may feel greater highs and greater lows, but you will also have an increased capacity to regulate these emotions without going into hyper- or hypoarousal. You'll have an expanded capacity for feelings, experiences, sensations, and aliveness.

Now that you have momentum, incorporating the practices you've learned into your daily routine will help keep you moving forward on the path of growth and healing. Here are some ways to keep your progress going:

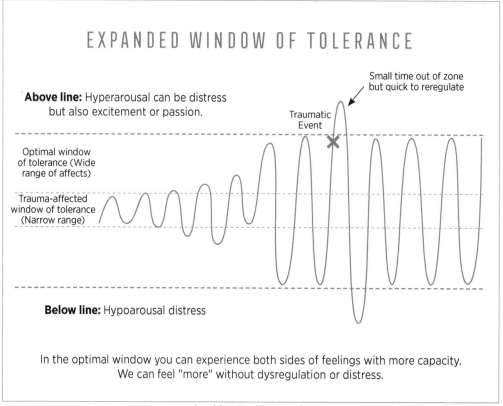

## EXPANDED WINDOW OF TOLERANCE

**Above line:** Hyperarousal can be distress but also excitement or passion.

Optimal window of tolerance (Wide range of affects)

Trauma-affected window of tolerance (Narrow range)

Traumatic Event

Small time out of zone but quick to reregulate

**Below line:** Hypoarousal distress

In the optimal window you can experience both sides of feelings with more capacity. We can feel "more" without dysregulation or distress.

*Adapted from Siegel, 1999; Ogden, Minton, and Pain, 2006; Ogden and Fisher, 2015.*

**PLAN AHEAD.** Continue to use your daily activity calendar (see chapter 5) to make time for self-care, and add to it as you develop new resources. Schedule both self-care activities and activities that involve other people.

**MAKE TIME FOR REFLECTION.** Review the many reflective and meditative exercises in this book, and remember to schedule time for your favorites. Taking time to pause is an important tool for self-regulation.

**SEEK THE POSITIVE.** The human brain has a tendency to focus on the negative, so we have to be diligent and mindful in noticing the positive—opportunities for gratitude, moments of joy or of beauty—in order to be able to fully experience them.

**BE GENTLE AND POSITIVE.** Now that you've practiced communicating with yourself, you can be your own best supporter. Give yourself lots of positive self-talk: words of encouragement, gentle pushes to remind yourself of the vision of change you're following. When your inner critic pops up, challenge that with your new beliefs and your new voice. Motivate yourself with simple affirmations when you need them: *I can do this! I am not my past. I can ask for help. I'm lovable just the way I am!*

**CREATE REMINDERS.** When life gets busy, set up external reminders to keep up with your self-care. Place sticky notes where you'll see them, set reminders on your phone, or set a regular check-in time with a friend so you can share support, encouragement, and accountability. Use healthy, feel-good activities—a walk, a bath, a song, a movie, a visit with a friend—as rewards for meeting goals.

# MY ROAD MAP TO GROWTH

In this exercise, you'll reflect on some of your main takeaways from your journey so far, and you'll begin developing a plan to continue using what you've learned. This is instrumental in reinforcing your healing process.

Take some time to browse through the workbook exercises, noting the most meaningful and salient points throughout your journey so far, then answer the questions below.

What are some of the key points you noticed as you reviewed your exercises?

_____

_____

_____

_____

_____

What are some of the new things you've learned about yourself while working in this book?

_____

_____

_____

_____

_____

What are some of the most important things you've learned about how intergenerational trauma has affected you?

_____

What are your goals for continued growth?

What are some of the ways you will support your efforts to achieve your goals?

What might interfere with your goals?

What might help you overcome these challenges and obstacles?

_____

_____

_____

_____

_____

What have been some of the most helpful tools so far?

_____

_____

_____

_____

_____

What changes have you noticed since you started with this book?

_____

_____

_____

_____

_____

What are you grateful for in your life?

_____

_____

_____

_____

_____

Keep this page where you can easily access it so you can remind yourself of your goals and next steps. Read them out loud to offer yourself a sense of empowerment. This increases the likelihood that you will make your goals happen.

## AFFIRMATIONS FOR SELF-GROWTH

In order to change the emotional template that you developed through intergenerational trauma, it's helpful to feed yourself positive words and experiences that may have been lacking in your life. Affirmations are one way to do this. Negative thoughts often lead you to more negativity in general; positive thoughts can move you toward more positive experiences. When you teach your mind to think and feel a positive thought, it helps create or deepen new neural pathways to replace the maladaptive habits created by trauma.

In an affirmation, you state your goals as if they have already happened. Repeating it can override the old, unhealthy messages of trauma and help you stay focused on the positive. When you repeatedly tell yourself you can't do something, you naturally begin to believe that you can't do it and therefore become afraid to try. When you repeatedly tell yourself you can do something, you're more likely to actually do it.

Below are some positive affirmations to choose from. You can also create your own.

Stand in front of a mirror and look into your own eyes, or, if that's difficult for you, focus your vision on an object in the room. Choose three affirmations from the list below, and repeat each one to yourself three times. After each repetition, pause and notice what feelings, physical sensations, and thoughts arise.

- *I deserve to be happy. I choose to be happy.*

- *I am loving. I am lovable.*

- *I am not my past. I can create my future.*

- *I can notice the sensations of my body with understanding.*

- *My emotional states can be changed and regulated.*

- *I can receive love from others. I can give love to others. I can give love to myself.*

- *I can communicate with intention.*

- *I can pause and reset when I am dysregulated.*

- *I am my own person. I am not my parents. I am not my grandparents.*

- *What happened to me does not define me.*

- *I am capable of building strong, healthy relationships.*

- *I am a work in progress, I am compassionate with myself.*

- *I can be safe in the world.*

- *I can detach from people, places, and things that harm me.*

- *I value the process more than the product.*

- *I can always find something to be grateful for.*

- *I choose to flow with peace and send it into the world to share with others.*

Repeat three chosen affirmations daily. Notice after a few days if you're starting to feel differently. Are you noticing more positive regard toward yourself and others? Some of these affirmations may feel foreign or untrue at first, incongruent with deeply held negative beliefs. But, with repetition, they can become more comfortable and can take their rightful place in your heart. Be gentle with yourself and keep going—you are on your way to embodying a new and brighter future.

# WHAT TO DO IF YOU'RE STILL IN DISTRESS

At this point in your journey, you may have a new sense of hope, having gained some insights and useful tools for dealing with trauma. However, you may still be experiencing distress and challenges. This is not unusual. Working through intergenerational trauma, or trauma of any kind, is not to be taken lightly. As we've talked about throughout this workbook, because of the deeply rooted nature of trauma, healing takes time. Your brain is working to create new neural pathways that allow new ways of thinking, understanding, feeling, and sensing.

This workbook is a tool, but it is not meant to take the place of therapy and other forms of support. The best support can be offered by a trauma-focused therapist and/or a self-help group that focuses on some of your specific symptoms. It's also valuable to ask for support from trusted family members or friends. Joining meditation/mindfulness, yoga, exercise, art, or other special interest groups can also bring valuable additional support and self-care. If you have a spiritual or religious community, you may find support there.

Here's some information to help you find resources to continue your healing journey.

## WORK WITH A THERAPIST

Finding and working with a therapist can be an important part of your journey; finding the right therapist for your situation is key. As we noted in chapter 2, it's important to find a relational trauma-informed therapist. The trauma-informed approach to therapy looks at everything through a trauma lens, understanding how symptoms are related to intergenerational trauma. A trauma-focused therapist will consider how the body and mind work together and will have the skill to be able to address both.

There are different therapeutic approaches to healing trauma. Some focus more on thoughts, and others focus on emotions and sensations. We believe the best therapy should integrate both approaches and include growth promotion. That is, the goal should go beyond symptom reduction to enable you to grow your "true self," to become more in tune with your aliveness, your vision, and your sense of curiosity. This growth gives you mental flexibility and a greater capacity for healthy relationships.

Some types of therapy are short-term and used for symptom reduction; other therapy types operate over a longer period of time and go beyond symptom reduction, fostering and promoting growth. It's our belief that, when working with the deep roots of intergenerational trauma, longer-term, growth-promoting therapy is important in enabling a new way for you to be in the world. Trauma is peeled off in layers, like taking off the leaves of an artichoke until you get to the heart. It will take time and effort, but the results can be spectacular.

When seeking a trauma therapist, you can ask for a phone consultation first to see if they're a good fit. Most often, this would be a 15-minute phone call. Ask about the prospective therapist's specific training in trauma and the type of therapy modality they're trained in (we mentioned some common types in chapter 1). Ask if the therapist has experience with clients who have your specific type of trauma, and ask how they would work with your case. Remember that the relationship between you and your therapist is one of the most important factors in successful therapy. An attuned therapist can pay attention to explicit and implicit communication, which is so important to healing.

If you need to go in-network for therapy, you can contact your health insurance company and ask for a trauma therapist.

## SUPPORT GROUPS

A support group experience can show you that you are not alone, and in a community of others who have shared similar experiences, you can learn from each other. Trauma- or PTSD-specific support groups can be especially helpful; some may focus on specific types of trauma, like sexual assault or domestic violence. It's a good idea to start your healing journey with groups that focus more on skill-building and stabilization than on processing trauma. Most important is a skilled group facilitator who can manage the group experience.

There are different types of support groups; some are peer led, some are therapist led, some are 12-step, others are offered by spiritual organizations. See Resources at the end of this book for a list of options.

We recommend that you try a few before you make your decision. Some people find that a group specific to their issues is the best fit; for others, a group that is more general—perhaps a group dealing with women's issues or one focused on breathwork or meditation—feels better.

## MORE THAN JUST ME

In this exercise, you will explore your current support network and any roadblocks that might prevent you from seeking more help for your healing journey.

Answer the questions in the space provided.

How has it felt using this workbook as a start to or part of your journey of healing?

_____

_____

_____

_____

What kinds of support do you currently have?

_____

_____

_____

_____

What additional kinds of support do you think might benefit you?

_____

_____

_____

_____

What are the messages you tell yourself that might hinder you from finding more help?

_____

_____

_____

_____

What may interfere with seeking a therapist?

_____

_____

_____

_____

What may interfere with finding a support group?

_____

_____

_____

_____

What are your daily strategies for connection with others?

_____

_____

_____

_____

Remember, actually scheduling something will make it more likely to happen. Give yourself some target dates to explore and connect with the best kind of additional support for you.

## PUTTING IT ALL TOGETHER

Congratulations on making it through the workbook. We hope it has been an amazing journey so far, and we hope you feel proud of yourself!

In this final exercise, we'd like to help you install all you've learned; that is, to internalize and really make it your own.

Think about your journey, and revisit your responses in the exercise My Road Map to Growth (page 160). Then, follow these steps:

1.  Settle down in a comfortable spot.

2.  Begin to notice your breath.

3.  Ground yourself in the present moment through your breathing; feel your feet on the floor and your body in the seat. Allow your spine to gently stretch and your breath to deepen.

4.  Visualize one of the items from your road map, or focus on this thought: *I have changed, I have been on a healing journey*.

5.  Notice what you feel inside. Notice the sensations; notice what you feel in your body, in your heart, and any images or colors that come to mind.

6.  Visualize something you may be grateful for. What sensations and feelings do you notice? Do you feel expansion?

7.  If you notice an uncomfortable sensation, move your attention to another area that feels more neutral or positive.

8.  Come back into the moment and see if you can continue to notice positive sensations.

9.  When you feel ready, gently bring your attention back to your surroundings.

Our hope is that you will live the tenets of this workbook—that you will create a list of things you are grateful for and repeat them as affirmations, follow your activity calendar, use your mindfulness and meditations, find ways to feed your soul, practice self-care, eat good food, exercise fully, sleep well, and remember the importance of seeking additional support. We believe that, through these actions, you will feel healthier, more joyful, more curious, more loving, and more alive. We thank you with all our hearts for joining us on this journey. We hope for you to continue and make this your ongoing journey of continued healing.

# CHAPTER HIGHLIGHTS

- Healing doesn't happen overnight; it takes time to develop new ways of interacting with the world and with yourself.

- There can be obstacles along the way, but don't let this discourage you. Remember that healing is a marathon, not a sprint.

- When you expand your window of tolerance, you increase the ability to feel all of your emotions.

- Therapy can focus on symptom reduction and also promoting growth.

- You can increase motivation through a daily calendar, self-affirmations, and help from family and friends; you don't have to do this alone.

- It's important to use other resources, such as therapy and self-help groups, to increase your growth and expansion.

- The journey doesn't end here!

# RESOURCES

## FINDING A THERAPIST

These organizations have directories and search tools that you can use to locate a therapist in your area.

- American Psychological Association psychology help center: APA.org/helpcenter

- Anxiety and Depression Association of America find a therapist directory: members .ADAA.org/page/FATMain

- International Society for Traumatic Stress Studies public resources: ISTSS.org /public-resources

- *Psychology Today* find a therapist search tool: PsychologyToday.com

## INTERGENERATIONAL TRAUMA TREATMENT MODALITIES

These websites provide information on various trauma-informed treatment methods. Most have links to therapists trained in these modalities.

- Dialectical Behavior Therapy: BehavioralTech.org

- Eye Movement Desensitization and Reprocessing International Association: EMDRIA.org

- Laurel Parnell Institute (Attachment-Focused Eye Movement Desensitization and Reprocessing): ParnellEMDR.com

- NeuroAffective Relational Model Training Institute: NARMTraining.com

- NeuroAffective Touch: NeuroAffectiveTouch.com

- Right Brain Psychotherapy Institute: RightBrainPsychotherapy.com

- Sensorimotor Psychotherapy Institute: SensorimotorPsychotherapy.org

- Somatic Experiencing Trauma Institute: TraumaHealing.org

- Trauma Resource Institute: TraumaResourceInstitute.com

- United States Association for Body Psychotherapy: USABP.org

## MENTAL HEALTH

These are informational websites on mental health and mental health disorders.

- Child Mind Institute: ChildMind.org/audience/for-families

- HelpGuide mental health and wellness: HelpGuide.org

- International Society for the Study of Trauma and Dissociation: ISST-D.org

- International Society for Traumatic Stress Studies: ISTSS.org/home

- National Alliance on Mental Illness: NAMI.org/Home

- National Center for Victims of Crime: VictimsOfCrime.org

- National Child Traumatic Stress Network: NCTSN.org/resources/what-child
  -traumatic-stress

- National Institute on Drug Abuse: DrugAbuse.gov

- National Institute of Mental Health: NIMH.NIH.gov/index.shtml

- National Suicide Prevention Lifeline: SuicidePreventionLifeline.org

- Substance Abuse and Mental Health Services Administration (877-SAMHSA-7):
  SAMHSA.gov

- Wounded Warrior Project: WoundedWarriorProject.org

## SUPPORT GROUPS

- Adult Children of Alcoholics: AdultChildren.org

- Al-Anon Family Groups automated meeting information (800-344-2666): Al-Anon.org

- Alcoholics Anonymous: AA.org

- Co-Dependents Anonymous International: CoDA.org/find-a-meeting

- Gamblers Anonymous: GamblersAnonymous.org/ga/locations

- Narcotics Anonymous: NA.org

- *Psychology Today* Find a Trauma and PTSD Support Group: PsychologyToday.com /us/groups/trauma-and-ptsd

- Self-Management and Recovery Training (SMART): SmartRecovery.org

- Sex and Love Addicts Anonymous: SLAAFWS.org

## HOTLINES

- Child Abuse: The Childhelp National Child Abuse Hotline: 800-422-4453

- Crisis Text Line: CrisisTextLine.org; text HOME to connect with a crisis counselor: US: Text 741741

- Domestic Violence: National Domestic Violence Hotline/Child Abuse/Sexual Abuse: 800-799-7233

- Family Violence Prevention: Family Violence Prevention Center: 800-313-1310

- National Eating Disorders Association helpline: 800-931-2237

- National Institute on Drug Abuse Hotline: 800-662-4357

- National Sexual Assault Telephone Hotline: 800-656-4673

- Substance Abuse and Mental Health Services Administration National Helpline: 800-662-4357

- Suicide Hotline: 800-273-TALK (273-8255)

- United Way; help finding services: 211.org and enter your zip code

- Veterans Crisis Line: 800-273-8255 and press 1 or text 838255; VeteransCrisisLine.net

## MINDFULNESS

- Greater Good Science Center at the University of California, Berkeley: greatergood .Berkeley.edu/topic/mindfulness

- Harvard University Health Services Center for Wellness and Health Promotion: wellness.huhs.Harvard.edu/home

- InsightLA: InsightLA.org

- Mindful Communications; Healthy Mind, Healthy Life: Mindful.org/author /jon-kabat-zinn

- UCLA Health Mindful Awareness Research Center: UCLAHealth.org/marc /mindful-meditations

- Smartphone Apps:

  » Buddhify: Buddhify.com

  » Calm: Calm.com

  » Headspace: Headspace.com

  » iChill: TraumaResourceInstitute.com/ichill

  » Insight Timer: InsightTimer.com

  » Smiling Mind: SmilingMind.com.au

# REFERENCES

Abrams, M. S. "Intergenerational Transmission of Trauma: Recent Contributions from the Literature of Family Systems Approaches to Treatment." *American Journal of Psychotherapy* 53, no. 2 (1999): 225.

Agin, D. P. *More Than Genes: What Science Can Tell Us About Toxic Chemicals, Development, and the Risk to Our Children.* Oxford, UK: Oxford University Press, 2010.

Ainsworth, Mary D. Salter. *Infancy in Uganda: Infant Care and the Growth of Love.* Baltimore, Md.: Johns Hopkins Press, 1967.

American Psychiatric Association. *Diagnostic and Statistical Manual of Mental Disorders DSM-5.* Fifth ed. Washington: American Psychiatric Press, 2013.

American Psychiatric Association. "Cognitive Processing Therapy." 2017. APA.org/ptsd-guideline /treatments/cognitive-processing-therapy.

Bar-On, D., J. Eland, R. J. Kleber, et al. "Multigenerational Perspectives on Coping with the Holocaust Experience: An Attachment Perspective for Understanding the Developmental Sequelae of Trauma Across Generations." *International Journal of Behavioral Development* 22, vol 2 (1998): 315–38.

Bartholomew, K., and L. M. Horowitz. "Attachment Styles among Young Adults: A Test of a Four-Category Model." *Journal of Personality and Social Psychology* 61, no. 2 (1991): 226–44. DOI.org/10.1037/0022-3514.61.2.226.

Beck, Aaron T. *Cognitive Therapy and the Emotional Disorders.* New York: Penguin, 1979.

Behavioral Tech. "What Is Dialectical Behavior Therapy?" BehavioralTech.org/resources/faqs /dialectical-behavior-therapy-dbt.

Bloch, D. *Words That Heal: Affirmations and Meditations for Daily Living*. Portland, Ore.: Pallas Communications, 1988.

Bowlby, J. *Attachment & Loss Vol. 1: Attachment*. New York: Basic Books, 1969.

Bromberg, P. *The Shadow of the Tsunami: And the Growth of the Relational Mind*. New York: Routledge, 2011.

Burns, D. D. *Feeling Good: The New Mood Therapy*. New York: HarperCollins, 1980.

Burton, N. "The 10 Golden Rules of Communication." *Psychology Today*. PsychologyToday.com /us/blog/hide-and-seek/201207/the-10-golden-rules-communication.

Carey, B. "Can We Really Inherit Trauma?" *New York Times*, Dec. 10, 2018. NYTimes.com /2018/12/10/health/mind-epigenetics-genes.html.

Centers for Disease Control and Prevention. "Preventing Adverse Childhood Experiences—ACES." 2019. CDC.gov/violenceprevention/pdf/preventingACES.pdf.

Centers for Disease Control and Prevention. "About the CDC-Kaiser ACE Study." 2020. CDC.gov/violenceprevention/acestudy/about.html?CDC_AA_refVal=https%3A%2F%2F.

Cherry, Kendra. "The Age Old Debate of Nature vs Nurture." Very Well Mind. 2020. VeryWellMind.com/what-is-nature-versus-nurture-2795392.

Collins, K., K. Connors, S. Davis, A. Donohue, S. Gardner, E. Goldblatt, A. Hayward, L. Kiser, F. Strieder, and E. Thompson. "Understanding the Impact of Trauma and Urban Poverty on Family Systems: Risks, Resilience, and Interventions." National Child Traumatic Stress Network. 2010. NCTSN.org/resources/understanding-impact-trauma-and-urban-poverty-family-systems-risks-resilience-and.

Danieli, Y. *International Handbook of Multigenerational Legacies of Trauma*. New York: Plenum, 1998.

DeAngelis, T. "The Legacy of Trauma: An Emerging Line of Research Is Exploring How Historical and Cultural Traumas Affect Survivors' Children for Generations to Come." *Monitor on Psychology* 50, no. 2 (2019). APA.org/monitor/2019/02/legacy-trauma.

de Bellis, M. D. "Developmental Traumatology: The Psychobiological Development of Maltreated Children and Its Implications for Research, Treatment, and Policy." *Development and Psychopathology* 13, no. 3 (2001): 539–64.

EMDRIA (Eye Movement Desensitization and Reprocessing International Association). "About EMDR Therapy." EMDRIA.org/about-emdr-therapy.

Fisher, J. "Dissociative Phenomena in the Everyday Lives of Trauma Survivors." Paper presented at the Boston University Medical School Psychological Trauma Conference. May 2001.

Fisher, J. *Healing the Fragmented Selves of Trauma Survivors: Overcoming Internal Self-Alienation.* New York: Routledge, 2017.

Freyd, J. J. *Betrayal Trauma: The Logic of Forgetting Childhood Abuse.* Cambridge, Mass: Harvard University Press, 1996.

Friedman-Gell, L. (2006). "Narcotics Anonymous: Promotion of Change and Growth in Spiritual Health, Quality of Life and Attachment Dimensions of Avoidance and Anxiety in Relation to Program Involvement and Time Clean." (doctoral thesis). Alliant International University, California School of Professional Psychology, Los Angeles.

Gornall, A. "Loving-Kindness Meditation." Dalai Lama Center for Peace and Meditation. DalaiLamaCenter.org/blog-post/loving-kindness-mindfulness-practice-instructions -heart?utm_source=%3E+Dalai+Lama+Center+Subscribers&utm_campaign=0c906bc903 -EMAIL_CAMPAIGN_2017_03_21_COPY_01&utm_medium=email&utm _term=0_82bc946c0d-0c906bc903-9711013.

Grohol, J. M. "15 Common Cognitive Distortions." Psych Central. PsychCentral.com/lib/15 -common-cognitive-distortions.

Hall, P. "Rules for Effective Communication." Dummies. 2020. Dummies.com/relationships /rules-for-effective-communication.

Herum, Alison M. "Families in Psychiatry: Preventing the Intergenerational Transmission of Trauma." *Clinical Psychiatry News.* 2013. MDedge.com/psychiatry/article/57864 /preventing-intergenerational-transmission-trauma.

Heller, L., and A. LaPierre. *Healing Developmental Trauma: How Early Trauma Affects Self-Regulation, Self-Image, and the Capacity for Relationship.* Berkeley, Calif.: North Atlantic Books, 2012.

Herman, J. L. *Trauma and Recovery.* Third ed. New York: Basic Books. 2015.

Holinger, P. C. "Your Baby's Earliest Feelings." *Psychology Today.* 2009. PsychologyToday.com/us /blog/great-kids-great-parents/200905/i-your-babys-earliest-feelings.

"How to Help Your Clients Understand Their Window of Tolerance." [Infographic] 2019. National Institute for the Clinical Application of Behavioral Medicine. NICABM.com /trauma-how-to-help-your-clients-understand-their-window-of-tolerance.

Kabat-Zinn, J. *Mindfulness for Beginners: Reclaiming the Present Moment and Your Life*. Boulder, Colo.: Sounds True, 2012.

Kabat-Zinn, J. *Full Catastrophe Living: Using the Wisdom of Your Body and Mind to Face Stress, Pain, and Illness*. New York: Random House, 2009.

Katehakis, A. *Sex Addiction as Affect Dysregulation: A Neurobiologically Informed Holistic Treatment*. New York: W. W. Norton & Company, 2016.

Kellerman, N. P. "Psychopathology in Children of Holocaust Survivors: A Review of the Research Literature." *Israeli Journal of Psychiatry and Related Sciences* 38, no. 1 (2001): 36–46.

Kohn, D. "Increased Stress in Fathers Leads to Brain Development Change in Offspring." University of Maryland School of Medicine. 2018. Medschool.UMaryland.edu/news/2018 /Increased-Stress-on-Fathers-Leads-to-Brain-Development-Changes-in-Offspring.html.

Leahy, R. L. *Cognitive Therapy Techniques: A Practitioner's Guide*. Second edition. New York: Guilford Press, 2017.

Lehrner, A., and R. Yehuda. "Cultural Trauma and Epigenetic Inheritance." *Development and Psychopathology* 30, no. 5 (2018): 1763–77.

Levine, P. A. *Waking the Tiger: Healing Trauma*. Berkeley, Calif: North Atlantic Books, 1997.

Levine, P. A. *Healing Trauma: A Pioneering Program for Restoring the Wisdom of Your Body*. Boulder, Colo.: Sounds True, 2008.

Levine, P. A. *In an Unspoken Voice: How the Body Releases Trauma and Restores Goodness*. Berkeley, Calif: North Atlantic Books, 2010.

Linehan, M. *DBT Skills Training Manual*. New York: Guilford Press, 2015.

Main, M., and J. Solomon. "Discovery of an Insecure-Disorganized/Disoriented Attachment Pattern: Procedures, Findings and Implications for the Classification of Behavior." In: T. B. Brazelton and M. W. Yogman, eds. *Affective Development in Infancy*. Norwood, N.J.: Ablex, 1986: 95–124.

Main, M. "Introduction to the Special Section on Attachment and Psychopathology: 2. Overview of the Field of Attachment." *Journal of Consulting and Clinical Psychology* 64, no. 2 (1996): 237–43.

Manfredi, D. Howtobehappy.Guru/positive-affirmations-a-simple-but-effective-exercise-that -can-improve-our-life/#how-to-create-positive-affirmations.

Marks-Tarlow, T. *Clinical Intuition in Psychotherapy: The Neurobiology of Embodied Response.* New York: W. W. Norton & Company, 2012.

Marks-Tarlow, T., M. Solomon, and D. Siegel. *Play and Creativity in Psychotherapy.* New York: W. W. Norton & Company, Inc., 2018.

McEwen, B. S. "The Neurobiology of Stress: From Serendipity to Clinical Relevance." *Brain Research* 886, nos. 1–2 (2000): 172–89.

Miller-Karas, E. *Building Resilience to Trauma: The Trauma and Community Resilience Models.* New York: Routledge, 2015.

Miller-Karas, E., and L. Grabbe. "The Trauma Resiliency Model: A 'Bottom-Up' Intervention for Trauma Psychotherapy." *Journal of the American Psychiatric Nurses Association.* 1–9. 2017. ACEsConnection.com/g/Parenting-with-ACEs/fileSendAction/fcType/0 /fcOid/480528347488215112/filePointer/480528347488215138/fodoid /480246307034100746/JAPNA%2012-2017%20TRM.pdf.

Narvaez, D. F., and D. Roy. "Solving Humanity's Emotional Disorders." *Psychology Today.* May 2015. PsychologyToday.com/us/blog/moral-landscapes/201505/solving-humanity -s-emotional-disorders.

Ogden, P. "Dissociation Then and Now." The International Society for the Study of Trauma and Dissociation. 2011, revised 2015. Facebook.com/notes/sensorimotor -psychotherapy-institute/dissociation-then-and-now-by-pat-ogden/526390140858597.

Ogden, P., and J. Fisher. *Sensorimotor Psychotherapy: Interventions for Trauma and Attachment.* New York: W. W. Norton & Company, 2015.

Ogden, P., and K. Minton. "Sensorimotor Psychotherapy: One Method for Processing Traumatic Memory." *Traumatology* 6, no. 3 (2000): 149–173.

Ogden, P., K. Minton, and C. Pain. *Trauma and the Body: A Sensorimotor Approach to Psychotherapy.* New York: W. W. Norton & Company, 2006.

Parnell, L. *Transforming Trauma: EMDR, the Revolutionary New Therapy for Healing the Mind, Clearing the Body, and Opening the Heart*. New York: W. W. Norton & Company, 1998.

Parnell, L. *Attachment-Focused EMDR: Healing Relational Trauma*. New York: W. W. Norton & Company, 2013.

Porges, S. W. *The Polyvagal Theory: Neurophysiological Foundations of Emotions, Attachment, Communication, and Self-Regulation*. First edition. New York: W. W. Norton & Company, 2011.

Porges, S. W. "Emotion: An Evolutionary By-Product of the Neural Regulation of the Autonomic Nervous System." *Annals of the New York Academy of Sciences* 807 (1997): 62–77.

Rakoff, V. M., J. Sigal, and N. B. Epstein (1966). "Children and Families of Concentration Camp Survivors." *Canada's Mental Health*, vol. 14, as noted in Tori DeAngelis, "The Legacy of Trauma." 2019.

Ryan, J., I. Chaudieu, M-L. Ancelini, and R. Saffery. "Biological Underpinnings of Trauma Post-Traumatic Stress Disorder: Focusing on Genetics and Epigenetics." *Epigenomics* 8, no. 11 (2016). FutureMedicine.com/doi/10.2217/epi-2016-0083.

Sartor, C. E., J. D. Grant, M. T. Lynskey, et al. "Common Heritable Contributions to Low-Risk Trauma, High-Risk Trauma, Post-Traumatic Stress Disorder, and Major Depression." *Archives of General Psychiatry* 69, no. 3 (2012): 293–99.

Scaer, R. C. *The Body Bears the Burden: Trauma, Dissociation, and Disease*. New York: The Haworth Press, 2001.

Schore, A. N. *Affect Regulation and the Origin of the Self: The Neurobiology of Emotional Development*. Mahwah, N.J.: Lawrence Erlbaum, 1994.

Schore, A. N. "The Effects of Relational Trauma on Right Brain Development, Affect Regulation, and Infant Mental Health." *Infant Mental Health Journal* 22 (2001): 201–69.

Schore, A. N. *Right Brain Psychotherapy*. New York: W. W. Norton & Company, 2019.

Schore, A. N. *The Development of the Unconscious Mind*. New York: W. W. Norton & Company, 2019.

Schore, J., and A. Schore. "Modern Attachment Theory: The Central Role of Affect Regulation in Development and Treatment." *Clinical Social Work Journal* 36, no. 1 (2008): 9–20. DOI: 10.1007/s10615-007-0111-7.

Shapiro, F. *Eye Movement Desensitization and Reprocessing EMDR Therapy: Basic Principles, Protocols, and Procedures*. New York: Guilford Press, 2001.

Shapiro, F. *Getting Past the Past: Take Control of Your Life with Self-Help Techniques from EMDR Therapy*. New York: Rodale Inc., 2012.

Siegel, D. J. *The Developing Mind: Toward a Neurobiology of Interpersonal Experience*. New York; Guilford Press, 1999.

Siegel, D. J. *Mind: A Journey to the Heart of Being Human*. New York: W. W. Norton & Company, 2017.

Stein D. J., K. C. Koenen, M. J. Friedman, et al. "Dissociation in Posttraumatic Stress Disorder: Evidence from the World Mental Health Surveys." *Biological Psychiatry* 73, no. 4 (2013): 302–12.

Stern, D. N. *The Interpersonal World of the Infant*. New York: Basic Books, 1985.

Tronick, E. Z., and M. K. Weinberg. "Depressed Mothers and Infants: Failure to Form Dyadic States of Consciousness." In L. Murray and P. J. Cooper, eds. *Postpartum Depression in Child Development*. New York: Guilford Press, 1997, 54–81.

Tull, M. "Dialectical Behavior Therapy (DBT) for PTSD." 2020. VerywellMind.com/dbt-for-ptsd-2797652.

Van der Hart, O., and M. Dorahy. "History of Trauma and Dissociation: Pierre Janet: The Pioneer on Trauma and Dissociation." *Automatisme psychologique*. Paris: Alcan, 1889. ESTD.org/history-trauma-and-dissociation.

Van der Hart, O., E. Nijenhuis, and K. Steele. *The Haunted Self: Structural Dissociation and the Treatment of Chronic Traumatization*. New York: W. W. Norton and Company, 2006.

Van der Kolk, B. A. "The Body Keeps the Score. Approaches to the Psychobiology of Posttraumatic Stress Disorder." In B. A. van der Kolk, A. C. McFarlane, L. Weisaeth, eds. *Traumatic Stress: The Effects of Overwhelming Experience on Mind, Body, and Society*. New York: Guilford Press, 1996, 214–41.

Van der Kolk, B. A. *The Body Keeps the Score: Brain, Mind, and Body in the Healing of Trauma*. New York: Penguin, 2014.

Van der Kolk, B. A., and R. E. Fisler. "Childhood Abuse and Neglect and Loss of Self-Regulation." *Bulletin of the Menninger Clinic* 58, no. 2 (1994): 145–68.

Winnicott, D. D. *The Child, the Family, and the Outside World.* Beverly, Mass.: Perseus, 1957.

Winnicott, D. D. *The Maturational Processes and the Facilitating Environment: Studies in the Theory of Emotional Development.* New York: Routledge, 1965.

Winnicott, D. D. *Babies and Their Mothers.* Beverly, Mass.: Perseus, 1987.

Winston, D. "How to Practice Relationship Building." 2016. Mindful.org/how-to-practice -relationship-building.

Yehuda, R. "Biological Factors Associated with Susceptibility to Posttraumatic Stress Disorder." *Canadian Journal of Psychiatry* 44, no. 1 (1999): 34–39.

Yehuda, R., S. L. Halligan, and L. M. Bierer. "Relationship of Parental Trauma Exposure and PTSD to PTSD, Depressive and Anxiety Disorders in Offspring." *Journal of Psychiatric Research* 35, no. 5 (2001): 261–70. PubMed.ncbi.nlm.nih.gov/11591428.

Yehuda, R., and A. Lehrner. (2018) "Intergenerational Transmission of Trauma Effects: Putative Role of Epigenetic Mechanism." *World Psychiatry* 17, no. 3 (2018): 243–57. NCBI.nlm.nih .gov/pmc/articles/PMC6127768.

# INDEX

# ACKNOWLEDGMENTS

We are thankful for those who have guided us along the way. First, we thank each other; neither of us could have gotten this far alone! We are truly a fifty-fifty partnership; we have opened a center and written this book together. We are full of love for each other and continue to inspire each other. Next, thank you to our amazing team at Callisto Media, most especially Seth Schwartz, Joe Cho, and Rick Chillot. We have many mentors in the field, our lighthouses in the eye of the storm: Dr. Allan Schore, Dr. Aline LaPierre, Dr. Janina Fisher, Dr. Laurel Parnell, Dr. Laurence Heller, and Dr. Pat Ogden—all experts we have been honored to study with. We have been strongly influenced by writers of literature on attachment, addiction, and trauma—too many to name. Thank you to Dr. Susan Swanson, Dr. Jennifer Schneider, Dr. Susan Krevoy, Dr. Kim Bergman, and our Allan Schore Study Group. We are grateful for the influences of Bill W. and Jimmy K. We thank and treasure friends, family, our Trauma and Beyond team, and our clients from whom we learn daily. Joanne sends special thanks to her husband, Anthony, her daughter Samantha, her parents, and her siblings, Donna, Joe, and Chuck. Lynne sends special thanks to her husband, Gary, her son, Jeremiah, her parents, sister Susie, and her fur babies.

# ABOUT THE AUTHORS

Psychologists **LYNNE FRIEDMAN-GELL, PHD,** and **JOANNE BARRON, PSYD,** are experts in the treatment of addiction and trauma. They became pioneers in the field by opening Trauma and Beyond Psychological Center®, an intensive treatment program specifically for sufferers of trauma. Both are trained in trauma resiliency model (TRM) therapy; they are both post-master's therapists in neuroaffective relational model (NARM); certified in eye movement desensitization reprocessing (EMDR), cognitive behavioral therapy, addiction counseling, psychodynamic psychotherapy, mindfulness, and neuroaffective touch; and both are currently pursuing ongoing training in interpersonal neurobiology, affect regulation, and sensorimotor psychotherapy.

Dr. Lynne received her PhD from the California School of Professional Psychology, followed by advanced studies at the Wright Institute Los Angeles. She also trained in infertility and reproductive issues in her postdoctoral work. At the center of her work is the mind-body-heart connection. Lynne was previously the clinical director of Insight Treatment Program and provides therapy, teaching, supervision, and consultation.

Dr. Joanne has a doctorate in clinical psychology and more than 40 years' experience in the mental health field. She was prominent in starting the first inpatient drug and alcohol program for teens in Los Angeles and was involved in developing several adult dual-diagnosis programs. She is a founding member of Women's Association of Addiction Treatment (WAAT), the founder of Adolescent & Young Adult Resource Network (AYARN), and cofounder of Insight Treatment Program.

CPSIA information can be obtained
at www.ICGtesting.com
Printed in the USA
JSHW042140250222
23361JS00001B/1